A BEGINNER'S
GUIDE TO

Online
Genealogy

A BEGINNER'S GUIDE TO

Online Genealogy

Learn How to Trace
Your Family History and
Discover Your Roots

MICHAEL DUNN

adamsmedia

AVON, MASSACHUSETTS

Published by
Adams Media, a division of F+W Media, Inc.
57 Littlefield Street, Avon, MA 02322. U.S.A.
www.adamsmedia.com

Contains material adapted and abridged from *The Everything® Guide to Online Genealogy*,
2nd Edition by Kimberly Powell, copyright © 2011, 2008 by F+W Media, Inc., ISBN 10:
1-4405-1168-3, ISBN 13: 978-1-4405-1168-4.

ISBN 10: 1-4405-8645-4
ISBN 13: 978-1-4405-8645-3
eISBN 10: 1-4405-8646-2
eISBN 13: 978-1-4405-8646-0

Printed in the United States of America.

10   9   8   7   6   5   4   3   2   1

Library of Congress Cataloging-in-Publication Data
Dunn, Michael,
  A beginner's guide to online genealogy / Michael Dunn.
     pages cm
  Includes index.
  ISBN 978-1-4405-8645-3 (pb) -- ISBN 1-4405-8645-4 (pb) -- ISBN 978-1-4405-
8646-0 (ebook) -- ISBN 1-4405-8646-2 (ebook)
  1. Genealogy--Computer network resources--Handbooks, manuals, etc. 2. Internet
research--Handbooks, manuals, etc. I. Title.
  CS21.5.D86 2015
  929.10285--dc23
                              2014038756

Cover design by Jessica Pooler.
Cover image © Oancea Catalin/123RF.

*This book is available at quantity discounts
for bulk purchases. For information, please
call 1-800-289-0963.*

Contents

Introduction

Are you curious about the origin of your last name? Confused as to why your grandfather never spoke about his family? Do you want to know if you have a famous relative or a bit of scandal in your background?

Years ago, you could have spent thousands of dollars and countless hours thumbing through piles of paper in a distant town or even foreign countries trying to get to the bottom of your family history. Fortunately, times have changed and, today, you can access millions of historical records from the comfort of your own home with just the click of a mouse. But how do you search through all that data to find what you really need? How do you find information on *your* family, when there's so much out there? That's where *A Beginner's Guide to Online Genealogy* comes into play.

Packed full of easy-to-understand, cost-effective ways to fill out your family tree, this book takes you through the process—step-by-step—and teaches you how to use the Internet to plan your project, track down your family (even if they lived overseas), and share your findings with other genealogists or even long-lost family members. You'll even find invaluable information on free databases, the most popular genealogy apps, and more—all from the comfort of your couch!

In addition, you'll learn how to use specialized software that makes it easy to keep track of hundreds or even thousands of tangled family connections. You'll see satellite images that can help you visualize the places where your ancestors once lived.

And you'll gain access to any number of online sites that can help you find military and death records, immigration passenger lists, and census reports to keep you moving forward.

As you search for your family history, you're guaranteed to make many discoveries along the way, both about your ancestors and about yourself. You may find that ancestors who led quiet, ordinary lives can be fascinating in their own special ways, and that history is much more interesting when you know that your ancestors were participants. And, once you learn about your family's history, you'll be able to guarantee that your ancestors' stories aren't lost to time by memorializing them on any number of genealogy sites or even by displaying a beautiful rendition of your family tree in your home. After all, their stories are your stories, so start researching and figure out who you really are. Enjoy the journey!

CHAPTER 1

Where Should You Begin?

Millions of digitized images, from marriage certificates to military service records, can be viewed online. Published genealogies allow budding family historians to extend their family tree by generations in just a few minutes. There is even free online software available to help you record the information you find and build your family tree. Today, you can successfully use the Internet to plug into your past. Before you begin, however, you first need to learn a few tools of the trade—the symbols, terms, and conventions used by genealogists to collect, record, and communicate the relationships in a family tree. Some of the information presented in this introductory chapter may seem a bit complex at first, but after you spend a little time tracing your family tree it will all start to come together.

Plan Your Project

Why are you interested in your family history? Are you curious about the origin of your last name? Do you want to learn more about Great-Grandpa's Polish roots? Are you hoping to identify as many of your ancestors as possible? Has an interesting story been handed down in your family that you want to pursue? Defining what you hope to learn on this journey is an important first step.

Even if your goal is to trace your entire family tree, it is practical to begin with one family line at a time. Otherwise, your research will quickly lead you into a bewildering maze of branching lineages. Go back just three generations in your own family tree, and you'll find yourself faced with researching the genealogy of eight great-grandparents. One family tree has now branched into eight, and it continues to multiply from there. By the time you've worked your way through ten generations of your family, you'll have discovered more than 1,000 ancestors!

Critical Clicks

As you research your family tree you may encounter numerous words with which you are unfamiliar—words specific to family history, as well as unfamiliar acronyms and legal and Latin terms commonly encountered in genealogical records. Look them up in online genealogy glossaries such as the ones listed under "Specialized Dictionaries for Genealogists" (*http://genealogy.about.com/od/glossaries*) on About.com Genealogy.

There are several different approaches you can take when beginning a family tree. A few of the more popular examples are detailed in the following sections, but pretty much anything related to researching something in the history of your family qualifies as genealogy. The format you choose to follow should be based on your individual research goals.

Direct Lineage

A direct lineage, alternately called a pedigree or ascendant tree, typically begins with you, a parent, or grandparent, and then follows a single surname or bloodline back through several generations in a direct line. This can also be expanded to include multiple direct lines, both of your parents, both of their parents, and so on. This is what most people think of when they refer to a family tree.

Family Lineage

Take the direct lineage family tree and throw in siblings; the siblings of your parents (your aunts and uncles), the siblings of your grandparents (your great-aunts and -uncles), and so on. This type of genealogy provides a more complete picture of the "family" going back through generations, rather than focusing only on the individuals from whom you directly descend.

Descendant Tree

A descendancy is the reverse of the traditional family tree. It usually starts with an ancestral couple pretty far back in the family tree and works forward to the present, attempting to account for all known descendants in all lines, both male and female. This is a popular approach for published family histories and for those looking to find relatives to plan a family reunion.

Collateral Genealogy

Basically an extension of the direct lineage, a collateral genealogy includes additional relatives who descend from the same common ancestor through lines other than your direct line, such as the spouses and children of siblings. This is similar to the descendant tree, except that most people use collateral genealogy as a type of "cluster" research approach (discussed in Chapter 2) to get around a brick wall in certain areas of their family tree, rather than because they are trying to document all descendants of a particular couple.

What's Next? Basic Research Steps

The typical family tree often ends up incorporating elements of most of the approaches discussed in the previous section, so just consider these as a starting point for your research. The point is to begin by selecting a particular individual, couple, or family line that you want to research. Once you've selected this starting point, genealogy research follows a fairly standard set of steps:

1. What do you want to know first? Review the information that you have collected to date to determine what you already know about your ancestor and what you still have left to learn. From there, select a fact that you want to uncover.

2. Identify a possible record or source for the information. If you want to learn a death date, you might want to search for a death record or obituary. If you're looking for the names of a couple's children, you may want to begin by searching for the family in the census.

3. Locate and search the record or source. Determine where and how you can access the record or source. Then search for your ancestor in the record. If you have trouble locating him or her, use the search strategies discussed later.

4. Record what you find (or did not find). Transcribe and/or extract the important details from the document or source, or make a photocopy. If it is a digital image or a web page, print a copy or save it to your computer. If the source does not contain information on your ancestor, make a note to that effect. Attach a full citation for the document or record to your research notes, as well as on any document copies.

5. Did you find what you were looking for? If you found the fact(s) you were looking for, move on to the next step. If not, go back to Step 2 and identify another source that may offer the information you hope to find. Since you can't always expect to find what you're looking for the first time, be prepared to cycle through Steps 2 through 5 several times.

6. Analyze and evaluate the new information. Look at how the fact you uncovered relates to what you already know. Does it answer your question? Does the new fact match up with everything else you know about the individual? Is the source a credible one? Use this new information to decide what you need to research next.

7. Organize and write as you go. If you don't write down where you found a particular piece of information, or add that printout to the pile of papers on your desk, you'll eventually find yourself overwhelmed. Your brain just can't hold it all. Most genealogists use research logs or genealogy software to keep track of the sources they've searched and the information they've found. You'll really appreciate this approach when you pick up your research after a few weeks or months away from it.

If you've answered the question you formulated in Step 1, select a new goal and begin the genealogical research process over again. If you haven't yet met your research goal, or feel that you need further evidence to support your findings, return to Step 2 and select a new record or source. If you've tried every source you can think of and still haven't found the answer you seek, don't get discouraged. At least you've learned where the answer isn't!

Collect Information

Written records are the foundation of genealogy research, documenting the vital events in an individual's life, from birth to marriage to burial. They also provide data on property ownership, military service, taxation, school attendance, census enumeration, memberships, and other important aspects of day-to-day life. These records, whether created by governments, organizations, or private institutions, are where you'll find many of the details about your ancestors. Documentary evidence of your relatives may also be found in other, less "official" sources, including newspapers, photographs, tombstones, family Bibles, school yearbooks, church membership lists, and even oral family histories.

A digital image that has been scanned or created from an original source is generally considered by genealogists as equivalent to the original as long as no evidence suggests that the image has been manipulated or altered, other than to enhance readability. Thus, there is generally no need to view both the microfilm and digitized version of the same record, unless there's a legibility issue or something appears to be missing.

The sources you'll encounter in your genealogy research can generally be classified, according to the Board for Certification of Genealogists (BCG), as either original or derivative. These are a little different from the terms "primary source" and "secondary source" that you may be used to, because they refer to the physical form and provenance of a document or record, not the information that it contains.

- An original source is one that exists as it was originally recorded. Examples might include an oral recorded history, a handwritten will, a baptism recorded in the church records, a diary, or a photograph.
- A derivative source is produced by reproducing some or all of the content contained in an original source. Photocopies, abstracts, extracts, transcriptions, databases, indexes, and authored works such as genealogies and histories are generally considered to be derivative sources, as is most information found on the Internet. Examples include a

transcript of an obituary, a database of marriage records, or a published genealogy.

Whenever possible, it is best to view the original source. Each time a record is transcribed, copied, or manipulated in some way there is a chance for errors to creep in. Handwriting can be difficult to interpret. Typographical errors are easy to make. Vital information can easily be skipped by accident or left out because it isn't considered important.

How reliable is information found on the Internet?
The majority of the records you'll deal with will be derivative sources, but this doesn't necessarily mean they are unreliable. It is best, however, to consider such information as a clue for further research, and not a statement of absolute fact. Look for a citation to the original source from which the information was derived so you can evaluate the source for yourself.

Most genealogists use the terms "primary" and "secondary" to classify information, rather than sources. This is because any single source may include both primary information and secondary information.

- Primary information is generally provided close to the time of an event, by someone with firsthand knowledge of the reported fact(s). A birth date recorded on the birth certificate by a doctor or parent present at the birth is an example of primary information.
- Secondary information is provided by someone with secondhand knowledge of the reported fact(s) or is information that was recorded long after the event occurred. A birth date recorded on a death certificate by a child of the deceased is an example of secondary information. This doesn't mean the information is incorrect, just that there is more of a chance that it could be.

Each fact or piece of information found within a source needs to be evaluated separately to determine whether it is primary or secondary. This classification doesn't refer to the accuracy of the information—it refers to the likelihood of its accuracy. The quality or weight of the information should also be further assessed based on who provided the information, knowledge of the informant, and how closely the information correlates with information provided by other sources. Secondhand information is often correct. And firsthand information can sometimes be inaccurate. A group of people who experienced a car accident firsthand, for example, will often tell slightly different versions of the story. In another case, a couple may have moved back their marriage date by a few months when they recorded it in the family Bible, to cover up an illegitimate birth.

Organize the Search

As your tree starts to bear fruit, you'll find that a computer can be of tremendous help in organizing your research and presenting your results. Some traditional organization of paper files and documents will still likely be necessary, but organization of your overall research is much more important, and this is where the computer can really shine. Not only does it take up much less space than piles of papers and boxes of documents, but a computer also makes it easier to search and sort through your family tree.

Critical Clicks

GEDCOM, an acronym for Genealogical Data Communication, is a special file format that can be read by most genealogy programs, allowing easy transfer of your family tree file from one program to the other. Learn how to open and read a GEDCOM file, as well as how to use your family tree program to create and share your own, in "Genealogy GEDCOM 101" (http://genealogy.about.com/od/family_tree_software/a/Genealogy-Gedcom.htm).

Download or Purchase a Genealogy Program

Family tree software is much easier to use than pencil and paper once your family tree begins to grow. Computer software allows you to type in the name, date, and other information on each individual just once; easily move back and forth between generations in your family tree; view and print a variety of reports on your ancestors; and exchange information with family members and other researchers. And since there are a number of good programs available for free, there really isn't a reason not to use genealogy software.

For those of you wondering which genealogy software is the best, there really isn't a clear-cut answer. Most genealogy programs today offer good, basic functionality, so your choice should really depend upon your individual goals and preferences. Some family tree software excels at publishing books or charts. Other programs do a better job at helping you organize and document your data. The best option is to try before you buy. Most companies that sell genealogy software have a website where you can download a free trial or demo version. Some programs, such as the standard versions of Legacy Family Tree and Family Tree Builder, as well as RootsMagic Essentials, are free. There are dozens of genealogy software programs available, but the following are some of the ones most widely used by genealogists that are still offering new versions and updates:

- Ancestral Quest (*www.ancquest.com*)
- Brother's Keeper (*www.bkwin.org*)
- DoroTree Jewish Genealogy Software (*www.dorotree.com*)
- Family Historian (*www.family-historian.co.uk*)
- Family Tree Builder (*www.myheritage.com/family-tree-builder*)
- Family Tree Maker (*www.familytreemaker.com*)
- Legacy Family Tree (*www.legacyfamilytree.com*)
- RootsMagic (*www.rootsmagic.com*)
- The Master Genealogist (*www.whollygenes.com*)

There are some excellent options for Macintosh users as well, including:

- Heredis Mac X.2 (*www.myheredis.com*)
- Family Tree Maker—Mac version (*www.familytreemaker.com*)
- Reunion (*www.leisterpro.com*)

A number of Internet-based family tree offerings allow you to create, view, and edit your family tree entirely online, an alternative to traditional standalone computer software. This is an excellent option for families or groups who are collaborating together on a genealogy, as well as for individuals who like to work on more than one computer. The most full-featured standalone option is Ancestry Member Trees (*http://trees.ancestry.com*), which allows you to build your family tree online from scratch (or GEDCOM upload), include notes and sources, and even attach documents (either records found on Ancestry .com or documents/photos uploaded from your own computer). Other online tools for building and sharing a family tree include MyHeritage (*www.myheritage.com/family-tree*), Geni (*www.geni.com*), and Family Pursuit (*www.familypursuit.com*). Most require some type of membership fee for full-feature use and none offer the tools, power, and flexibility of the best computer-based genealogy software programs.

Critical Clicks

Many of these genealogy programs—like RootsMagic—also offer free mobile apps that will help you enter information, wherever and whenever you need to. Go to the app store on your smartphone, search for "genealogy app," read the reviews, and choose a program that works for you.

Additional software options help you get your family tree information from your desktop genealogy program and then publish it online (usually via a GEDCOM file).

Keep a Research Log

Whether you keep it on paper or on your computer, a research log is essentially a place where you keep track of your research, from the planning stage through to completion—essentially a journal of your research process. You use it to record what you are planning to look for and where you plan to look for it. After you search the source, you add information about when you searched, what names and name variations you searched for, and what you did and did not find. You may also choose to include a record of any correspondence (e-mails, letters, and so on) in your research log, although some genealogists choose to maintain a separate correspondence log. You can track all of your research in one big research log, or maintain separate research logs for each individual, family group, or surname.

Right now, as you're just setting out on your family tree journey, a research log approach may seem like a waste of time. But chances are that after you've spent a few weeks and months researching online, you'll end up visiting the same places again and again. That's not to say that you shouldn't revisit websites. Most are continually adding new information, and you'll also keep discovering new ancestors to research. But unless you keep track of where you've been and who and what you've searched for, you can end up wasting a lot of time and effort retracing your previous trail.

You can find a variety of research log forms online for free download, or you can easily design your own. Many genealogy software programs also offer a simple to-do list or research log feature. The goal is to keep track of the research you've done and plan to do, and whatever format is the easiest for you to use and maintain is the one you should use.

Critical Clicks

Clooz is an electronic filing cabinet designed just for genealogists who prefer computer organization to paper files. It includes more than 100 templates for recording information found in a wide variety of different genealogical records, along with blank templates, source templates, and other methods of organizing the little scraps of data you come across when researching your family tree. You can download a free trial at *www .clooz.com.*

Take Good Notes

You don't want to have to rely on your memory for vital details, so consider using your computer or a notebook to take notes. Most genealogical software has a special space for notes on each individual, and some include a notes field for each individual event, as well. Always label your notes with the date and place where they were taken, as well as a complete reference, or citation, to the original source.

Part of taking good notes is learning how to copy the information you find in documents and other source materials. This copying can take a number of forms, but the three most common are transcripts, abstracts, and extracts.

- A transcript (transcription) is a complete, word-for-word copy of the original document. Everything is copied exactly as it appears, including any errors, misspellings, abbreviations, and punctuation. If something needs clarification or you want to include your interpretation of something, comments can be added in square brackets [like this], not in parentheticals. This convention tells other readers that you have added the information contained within the brackets, and that it was not found in the original.

- An abstract is a summary of a document's essential details, including names, dates, places, and events, in the same order that they appear in the original source. Nonessential words and punctuation are omitted. As with transcriptions, copy all names, dates, and abbreviations exactly as they appear in the original.

- Extracts are similar to abstracts in that they include only portions of the original document text. Instead of summarizing, however, an extract is an exact word-for-word copy of a selected portion of text, set off by quotation marks. Extracts can stand alone, but you'll more commonly find them included as part of an abstract to highlight essential portions of the text.

Even if you keep both digital and paper copies of original documents, such as wills and land deeds, it often helps to make a full transcription and include it in the notes section of your genealogy software, or with your research, for easy reference—a transcription is much easier to read quickly than old, faded handwriting. Transcriptions and abstracts are also useful for situations in which you can't make a copy of the original document.

Tame the Paper Monster

Even if you keep almost all of your genealogy research on the computer, you'll probably still have boxes and files of certificates, photocopies, photos, and other paper records generated during the course of your search. You can scan important documents and photos into your computer, of course, but even then you may not want to throw away the originals. Genealogists use a number of different systems for organizing their files, including folders, binders, and notebooks. You can find an overview of several common filing systems online—just type "genealogy organization" into your favorite search engine. The books *Organizing Your Family History Search* by Sharon DeBartolo Carmack and *The Organized Family Historian* by Ann Carter Fleming, CG, CGL, offer additional organization examples and advice.

Genealogical Guidance
While transcribing a document, if you feel the need to insert a comment, correction, interpretation, or clarification, include it in square brackets [like this], not parentheses, to avoid confusion. Bracketed question marks [?] can be substituted for letters or words that can't be interpreted, or for interpretations that are questionable.

Record Your Progress

A family tree is basically one big puzzle. If you don't put the puzzle pieces together in just the right way, you'll never get to see the final picture. To help fit all of the puzzling clues together, genealogists use a variety of charts and forms to record their research data. The chart most people begin with is the pedigree chart or ancestor chart. This chart begins with you, or the individual whose ancestry you're tracing, and then branches with each generation to display the line of your direct ancestors. Pedigree charts come in a wide variety of shapes, sizes, and styles. The most common is a four-generation chart on standard 8½" × 11" paper. Some charts squeeze five or six generations into the same space, but necessarily include less room for information about each ancestor. Large, wall-sized ancestor charts can be printed from many genealogy software programs and then cut and pasted together, or you can order a specially printed wall chart of your family tree from a chart printing service (great for family reunions).

The other commonly encountered genealogy form is the family group sheet. This form focuses on a family unit, with space for recording a couple and their children, including birth, death, and marriage events for each individual. Generally, these two forms work in conjunction. The pedigree chart provides the overall picture of the family tree, with links between generations, while the family group sheet records additional family details for each couple or marriage recorded on the pedigree chart.

Most genealogists follow certain standard conventions when recording data, whether on a paper chart or in their genealogy software program. By following these conventions, you help to ensure that the information you record is as complete as possible, easy to understand, and not open to misinterpretation.

Critical Clicks

A variety of free genealogy forms can be downloaded online for your personal use, including ancestor or pedigree charts, family group sheets, research logs, and census extraction forms. Family Tree Magazine (*www.familytreemagazine.com/forms/download.html*) and About.com Genealogy (*http://genealogy.about.com/od/free_charts*) offer a nice variety. Enter "genealogy charts" in your favorite search engine to find even more genealogy charts and forms.

Record Names in Their Natural Order

Enter the first name (also referred to as a given name or forename), followed by the middle name and surname or last name. Married women are recorded under the last name they were born with—their maiden name—not the last name they took when they got married. In situations where you wish to include both last names (such as in a written family history), you can enclose the maiden name in parentheses prior to the married name.

While it is not necessary, most genealogists record surnames in capital letters (THOMAS). This makes it easy to distinguish surnames at a glance when scanning pedigree charts or genealogy queries. If you're using genealogy software, it is usually better not to enter the surname in all caps, as most programs will allow you to choose how you want the names printed in charts or reports. Entering last names in initial caps lowercase (Thomas) allows for greater flexibility.

Naming conventions also exist for certain special situations. Again, if you're using genealogy software you won't need to worry about most of these.

- When a woman has married several times, enter her given name followed by her maiden name in parentheses, followed by the last name of her husbands in order of marriage. (Don't do this if you are using genealogy software, as you'll enter each marriage and husband separately and record the wife only under her maiden name.) Example: Linda Michelle (Koth) GARDNER MITCHELL.
- Enter nicknames in quotes, not parentheses, following the given name. Genealogy software generally offers a special field in which to enter nicknames. Example: Mary "Polly" JENNINGS.
- If an individual was known by more than one name because of adoption or name change, include the alternate name in parentheses following the surname. Precede the alternate name with "a.k.a." for "also known as." If you're using a genealogy program, look for a special alternate name field. Example: William Maxwell MILLS (a.k.a. William Maxwell CRISP).
- If the surname spelling has been changed, you can record the earlier surname first, followed by the more current usage. Alternately, you can just record the surname for each individual as he or she commonly spelled it. Example: Stanislaw TOMAN/THOMAS.

Record Dates Carefully to Avoid Confusion

In the United States, dates are written differently than in most other parts of the world. Americans are used to dates with the month first, followed by the day and year—as in July 9, 1971. In most other countries, the same date would be written as 9 July

1971, with the day first. Both dates are easy to understand when they are written out as in the preceding examples, but when you see a date written 7/9/71 do you interpret it as July 9, 1971, or September 7, 1971? Or could the year be 1871 or 1771? To avoid confusion in family histories, genealogists conventionally follow the day, month, and year format for all dates, with the year written out in full. Months are generally written out in full as well, although standard three-letter abbreviations may be used.

There will be plenty of occasions in your research when you will only have an approximate date for an event. In such situations you can specify the date as "about" (abt. 1890) or "circa" (c. 1890). If you are able to narrow a date down to a specific time span (e.g., your ancestor most likely died between the day when he signed his will and the date the will was admitted into probate), record the time span using the abbreviation "bet" (between) followed by the two dates separated by a hyphen, as in 23 May 1789–3 June 1789. You can also record an event as occurring before or after a specific date—for example, (bef. 18 Jan 1892) or (aft. 11 Sep 2001).

Record Places from the Smallest Jurisdiction to the Largest

In general, this would mean the name of the place (town, village, or city), followed by the county or parish in which it was located, and then the state or province. The county or parish can be set off by commas or included in parentheses, as in Pittsburgh, Allegheny County, Pennsylvania or Tarboro (Edgecombe), North Carolina.

The specific geographical divisions will be different in different countries and regions, but just apply the "smallest to largest" convention and you'll have it right. If your research is predominantly in one country, such as the United States, you don't need to record the name of that country, although you might want to record the country for locations outside of your predominant country of research to avoid confusion.

Document Your Findings

Gathering facts about your family and assembling them into a family tree is quite an accomplishment, but it is the backing up of these facts with sources that will give your research credibility. Keeping track of where you found each piece of information or statement of fact is important as a means for others to evaluate or verify your work. It also allows you to easily go back again and again, to remember where your information came from, or to confirm its reliability in your own mind. To do this, genealogists use what is called a source citation. The source is the document, database, photograph, interview, or other record in which the specific fact or information was found. The citation is the formal reference to that source, including all details necessary for someone to identify and locate the source material.

Source citations in genealogy generally follow standard bibliographic citation standards, similar to those found in *The Chicago Manual of Style*. A good rule of thumb is to work from general to specific.

- Author or compiler (the person who created the content)
- Title of the source (book, website, and so on)
- Publication details (place, publisher, and date)

- Specific details needed to locate the information within the source (page number, chapter, entry, and so on)

Internet sources generally follow the same format as traditional published materials. A website title, for example, is equivalent to a book title. A database contained within a specific website can be treated as a book chapter. The publisher is the entity that owns or created the website, although this can be omitted if it duplicates the name of the website, as it does with Ancestry.com. In place of traditional publication place and date, you cite the URL of the website and the date on which you accessed or viewed the site. The additional details necessary for a footnote citation would include the information necessary to find the actual record, such as the individual's name and location and the entry number.

A footnote source citation for a World War I Draft Registration Card found online at Ancestry.com might appear as follows:

"World War I Draft Registration Cards, 1917–1918," digital images, Ancestry.com (*www.ancestry.com*: accessed 13 December 2010), card for Claude Mancil Crisp, no. 2927, Edgecombe County, North Carolina; citing World War I Selective Service System Draft Registration Cards, 1917–1918, National Archives microfilm publication M1509, imaged from Family History Library film roll 1765639.

Sources will use slightly different punctuation and arrangement depending on how they are used—footnote, bibliography, or inline. This example is a bit complicated since it references digital images, but it also fairly represents many of the genealogical databases accessed online.

Cite what you see! Many of the sources you'll be using online, such as indexes, pedigree charts, and cemetery transcriptions, have been created or "derived" from a previously existing source. While such a derivative source may include a citation to the original source of the information, you must cite what you actually "see" or use—the derivative source, not the original from which it was created. This is because derivative sources are prone to human error, including typing mistakes and misinterpreted handwriting. If such a mistake exists and you cite the original source without reference to the online derivative source where you actually found your information, others will assume that the error is yours.

Consider a situation where you locate your great-grandmother's birth date from a transcription made and posted online by the local genealogical society. In this case, you would not cite her tombstone and/or the cemetery as your source because you have not personally seen her grave marker. Instead, you would cite the online transcription created by the genealogical society.

Many people don't take the time to cite sources when they first begin researching their family tree. It's just so easy to assume that all of your data is accurate, so why does it matter where it came from? It's also easy to get caught up in the excitement of the search and tell yourself that you'll go back and do it later. Problems arise, however, when you find new information that contradicts your previously "accurate" data. Without sources, you have no way to know where you found the earlier information, which makes it difficult to resolve the discrepancy. Documenting sources for all of the information as it is uncovered can save many, many hours of backtracking. Source citations really are worth the extra time and effort!

Know Where to Start

Now that you know how to record your data, it's time to start your search! And what better place to start than by asking your own relatives and writing down all the info you can find out before you begin your online search. Many people begin their family tree search knowing next to nothing about their own grandparents and great-grandparents. Sure, you know their names, and perhaps their date of birth, but do you know when they were married? What they did for a living? Where they lived when they were growing up or the names of their siblings? Without at least some basic knowledge of your family tree, you're likely to quickly find yourself spinning your wheels online. That's why a good genealogy search should always begin at home.

Question Your Family Members

There's nothing quite as deflating as calling your grandmother to share your latest genealogy "find" only to have her reply, "I could have told you that." Your family members represent a vast source of untapped knowledge about your family history, and questioning them will likely turn up countless interesting details. Contact everyone you can think of, from your ninety-eight-year-old great-grandma to the second cousin you haven't seen since you were kids. Even friends of the family can provide useful details.

Talking to your family members can mean anything from a formal recorded interview to a casual conversation over the dinner table, or even an occasional question asked by e-mail. The casual conversation approach works especially well, as it seems to put family members more at ease. The downside, however, is that you don't always get the chance to take notes right away, and have no recording to fall back on. A nice compromise is to set up a video camera on a tripod in the corner of the dining room or other room where the interviewee feels comfortable, and then start a casual conversation about family events and memories. Your subject will often forget the camera is running (or at least stop worrying about it). If you can get two or more family members together at once, the informal conversation and memory sharing pretty much takes care of itself. Either way, ask a few questions to get the conversation started, but don't be afraid after that point to let your relative(s) wander from one memory to the next.

Critical Clicks

Storycorps (*www.storycorps.com*) brings trained facilitators and high-quality recording equipment to locations around the country to help record interviews between friends and family, in which one person interviews the other. The recorded interviews are added to the StoryCorps Archive, housed at the American Folklife Center at the Library of Congress, and participants receive a broadcast-quality copy of their interview on CD.

Decide Who to Interview First

Begin by talking to the oldest living family members, when possible, because they are the ones whose memories are most at risk of being lost forever and they usually know the most about the family. You'll often find them the easiest to talk to as well, because they have more free time and usually appreciate the fact that someone is interested in their stories. It also helps to think about what you're hoping to learn and who is most likely to have that information. If your goal is to learn your great-grandmother's maiden name, you might want to start with your grandmother, if she is still living, or one of her siblings. Or you may just want to start with the people who are most willing or interested in the information you are gathering. It's a lot easier to get information from someone who is excited about what you are doing.

Most families also have at least one person known to be the keeper of the family history—the one who has spent some time researching the family tree, who has the largest collection of family photos and memorabilia, or is just the "busybody" sort who knows everything about everyone. This is someone you're definitely going to want to talk to. He or she may not always be someone in your direct line, however, so it may take some detective work on your part. If your great-grandfather, for example, had several siblings, then descendants of any of those other children are just as likely as your grandfather to have family photos, letters, and other items that have been saved.

There are many tutorials and guides online to help you prepare for and conduct a successful oral history interview, covering such matters as what to bring with you and which questions to ask for best results. More important than all these little details, however, is actually sitting down and talking to your relatives. To get you started, here are some basics to keep in mind:

- Check your equipment in advance. Be sure you have paper and pencil and extra batteries, and that the equipment all works. If you can get into the room where you're going to conduct the interview, do a practice run to be sure the microphone will pick up both you and the interviewee.
- Come prepared. Bring a list of topics you want to cover, family group sheets or pedigree charts to be verified or expanded, and some family photos and other props to help jog your relative's memory.
- Don't interrupt. The best way to keep your interviewee involved is to listen to what she has to say. You can ask follow-up questions to get more details, but don't worry too much about your interview getting off track as long as your relative is still talking about the family. Sometimes those little "tangents" reveal the most interesting clues.
- Be respectful, not pushy. If your relative appears reluctant to give details about a particular event or person, don't press. There may be a "secret" or a painful memory, and pushing too hard can mean an end to her willingness to talk to you.

Save it for a future conversation, or as something to ask other relatives about.

- Make note of any names, places, and events mentioned during the interview. After the interview, ask your relative to go through this list with you, to add full names with correct spellings.
- Follow through. If you taped the interview, make a transcript. If you took written notes, make a photocopy. Send a copy to your interviewee along with a thank-you letter.

While you're busy digging for facts to fill in the blanks of your genealogy software or family tree chart, don't forget to ask for and record the stories as well. Every family has them; some are well-rehearsed—like the stories Grandpa likes to tell just about every time the family gets together. Others may have never been told because no one ever thought to ask. Both are an important part of the family history and deserve to be written down.

Genealogical Guidance

Almost all family stories have a kernel of truth, but sometimes that's about all that's true. You may hear stories of being related to a famous individual, such as Abraham Lincoln or Napoleon Bonaparte. You may be told that your great-great-grandmother was a Cherokee princess. Or you may encounter the common tradition that your family tree goes back to "three brothers" who came to America. It's possible, of course, that these stories are true. It's much more likely, however, that such stories are more myth than fact.

Even if you've been asking your family members questions for years, they will still manage to surprise you with new information. Don't expect to learn everything the first time you ask, and don't listen when a family member tells you they don't know anything. It may take time, patience, and creativity, but you can generally learn something useful from every living relative in your family tree.

Ask Your Family for Genealogical Treasures

You might be surprised what lurks in the homes of your relatives. They may be surprised, too! Family history can be found in unusual places—the hem of a quilt, the back of a photo, a locket inscription. Photos and albums help match names with faces. If pictures aren't labeled, ask your relatives to help you with identification. Family Bibles often contain information about marriages, births, baptisms, deaths, and other important family events. Letters and postcards may be filled with family news and stories, and the date and postmark may provide clues as to where your family lived at a given time. If your family has been in the same home for generations, even the walls can talk. You may find notes recorded on the inside of closet doors, growth charts penciled on the walls, or old newspapers used for insulation in the attic. Ask your relative if they will agree to go through their house with you, as this allows you to easily ask questions about anything you find. If this isn't possible, however, here are some things you might ask your relative to look for:

- Important papers (birth certificates, wills, naturalization documents, titles, and deeds)
- Pictures, photo albums, scrapbooks, baby books
- Newspaper clippings
- Bibles
- Letters and postcards
- Diaries and journals
- Books (check for inscriptions)
- Funeral and Mass cards
- Family trees
- School papers, including report cards and yearbooks
- Awards and certificates
- Quilts, samplers, or other needlework
- Jewelry (check for inscriptions)

Your relatives may be understandably reluctant to let precious family records or mementos out of their possession, so consider bringing a portable scanner and a laptop with you on your attic hunt. A good digital camera can also do the trick. This way you'll have digital copies of everything for your records, and to easily share with the rest of the family. Take good notes, and transcribe any documents in case your pictures or scans don't turn out as well as expected.

Has this already been done?
Even if you can't locate someone in your immediate family who has researched the family history, it doesn't mean it hasn't already been done. Most family trees have many, many branches that have spread far and wide through successive generations. This means that records that detail your family may not always be found in the possession of your relatives, or even in the area where your ancestors lived. A written family history, a collection of old family letters, or a scrapbook of ancestral photographs may have been donated to a library or repository on the other side of the country, but how do you find it?

Don't Get Ahead of Yourself

Now that you have some sort of an idea what you're looking for, it may be very tempting to jump ahead of yourself and skip a generation or two. Imagine that you discover a census record for your grandmother living with her husband and children. But wait! You look further down and find her father living in the same household. Just think, you've learned your grandmother's maiden name and her father's name in one fell swoop. You're probably already typing his name into a search box to see what else you can learn! And then there's the tale your grandfather told of his father arriving at Ellis Island as a young man of eighteen with nothing more than the clothes on his back. One of the first things you're going to want to do online is search for him in the Ellis Island database, right?

Jumping ahead of oneself is human nature. But in genealogy it can also mean disaster. By skipping a generation or two, you run the risk of identifying the wrong people as your ancestors and being tangled forever in someone else's family tree. It happens more frequently than you may think. This doesn't mean you can't pursue a new lead when it smacks you in the face, but after you've done some searching to satisfy your curiosity, go back and finish your research on the previous generation(s) to ensure that everything does indeed match up as you believe. Don't just rely on your grandmother's name and the name of her father. Identify as much as you can about your grandmother, checking all of the available records for anything you can glean. Just learning something as simple as where and when she was born can help distinguish her from others of the same name. Additional research may also provide you with the names of siblings, the birthplace of her parents, her mother's name, and other clues. This way, when you locate records for her parents, you can feel confident that you have correctly identified the next branch in your family tree.

Genealogical Guidance

Naming patterns can sometimes help identify links between generations of a family. You may find names of grandparents, parents, aunts, and uncles repeated in succeeding generations. Occasionally you'll even find an unusual name that has survived in the family for decades. Sometimes an unusual middle name may indicate the maiden name of the mother or grandmother.

CHAPTER 2

Learn How to Search

One of the first things many would-be family historians do when they decide to peek into their family's past is type the name of their ancestor into a major search engine or genealogy database. After sifting through thousands of irrelevant results, they throw up their hands in frustration, convinced that nothing exists online about their family. The problem with this scenario, however, isn't the lack of information; it's the technique. Strong search skills are an essential tool for successful online genealogy research.

Search Engine Basics

You wouldn't wander aimlessly through the stacks at a large city library looking for a book on your family. In the same way, you shouldn't approach a family history hunt on the Internet without a plan. Whether you're using a search engine like Google or searching for your ancestors in the Ellis Island database, an important part of online genealogy research is learning how to search. The sheer magnitude of information available online makes locating information on a particular individual a bit more complicated than just typing a name into a search engine. There are three simple ways to improve your search results: (1) choose your search terms carefully, (2) learn how to use special search operators, and (3) restrict your search with special commands.

Other Facts Help Narrow the Search

It's always a good idea to think about your search before you begin. What do you know about your great-grandfather Jack Smith that can help you distinguish him from all the other Jack Smiths of the world? Perhaps you know that he was born in Monongahela, Pennsylvania. You also know that he married your grandmother, Cornelia, and that he was a blacksmith. Use these facts as keywords to help narrow down your search. A search for "JackSmith blacksmith Monongahela" or "Jack Smith Cornelia Monongahela" is much more likely to yield something about your great-grandfather than a search for just "Jack Smith."

For more general results, you might try adding the word "genealogy" or "family" to your surname, as in "Powell genealogy" or "Owens family." This type of search will often bring up family history information that other researchers have posted online. To be honest, this type of search technique lends itself better to names more unique than Powell or Owens. In the preceding example, better results were achieved when at least one more identifying keyword was added to the search, such as "Archibald Powell genealogy" or "Owens family Edgecombe NC."

> **Which search engine is best for genealogy?**
> Most genealogists prefer Google (*www.google.com*), primarily because it indexes the most pages and tends to return somewhat relevant results. Metasearch cluster engines Gigablast (*www.gigablast.com*) and Yippy (*www.yippy.com*) are also useful because they combine searches from a variety of sources and then help you narrow things even further with categorized results. Learn more about these and other search options in Wendy Boswell's excellent guide to the "*Best Search Engines on the Web*" (*http://websearch.about.com/od/enginesanddirectories/p/websearch101.htm*).

Along these same lines, consider what you want to find. If you're looking for death information, you'll want to try the word "death" or "died" in your search. You could also try adding the word "cemetery" or "obituary" to your search query to bring up death information about your ancestor. Think about the types of words that might appear in the information you're looking for, and use these as keywords to help focus your search.

Use Search Operators to Focus Results

Most major search engines, including Google, MSN, and Yahoo!, allow you to use special search operators to focus results. These operators allow you to search for specific phrases, exclude certain words, or otherwise fashion a search query that will help you find exactly what you want.

- Use quotation marks to find complete phrases. Regular searches look for all keywords to appear on the same page, but don't pay any attention to their proximity to one another. A search for *Jebediah Smith* would turn up a page that contained "Jebediah Brazelton" and "Bob Smith," neither of whom are your Jebediah Smith. By enclosing specific search phrases in quotes, you force the search engine to find documents that contain the exact phrase, as in "Jebediah Smith" or "Washburn Cemetery."
- Include the Boolean operators *AND* or *OR* between words. As it sounds, the Boolean operator AND used between two words tells the search engine that both terms must be present on the web page to be included in the search results. Most search engines assume an AND between keywords, or you can use the plus sign, so it isn't often necessary to use this command. The Boolean operator OR requires one term or the other to be present on a web page, but not both. This feature can be helpful when searching for name variations Powell AND Archie OR Archibald or when searching for variations of the same term Crisp AND tombstone OR gravestone. Boolean operators must be in ALL CAPS.

- Add a plus (+) to force certain words to be included in your search. The plus sign is rarely needed, but can serve as a substitute for AND to ensure that all of your keywords are included in the results. So, instead of using "crisp AND cemetery AND macclesfield" you could use "crisp +cemetery +macclesfield." There are also some small words, called "stop words," that search engines commonly ignore when processing a search query. If you really need these to be a part of your search, add a plus (+) in front of them, as in "Thomas Jefferson +will."
- Add a minus (–) to exclude specific words from your search. When your ancestor shares a name with a famous individual or a popular product, you can use this option to help direct the focus away from these irrelevant results. A search for "Jimmy Dean –sausage" will help eliminate results from the Jimmy Dean company, while Washington –DC –George –president will help eliminate at least some of the clutter caused by the millions of results for President George Washington.

Critical Clicks

Specialized genealogy directories and search engines can help you find genealogy-specific sites without having to wade through as many irrelevant results. Cyndi's List (www.cyndislist.com) is the best of the bunch with over a quarter of a million links to online genealogical resources, organized into 180+ categories. Cyndi Howells, the woman behind Cyndi's List, has been maintaining this essential site for genealogists since 1996. Linkpendium (www.linkpendium.com) is another good specialized genealogy directory.

Restrict Your Search with Special Commands

As you get more comfortable with simple searches, you might want to try your hand at more advanced techniques. Most major search engines include special commands that allow you to restrict your search in some way—to a specific site or date range, for example. The list of available search commands varies by search engine, but the most useful for genealogy purposes is the "site:" command, which restricts your search results to a specific website or domain. The search command "James Brown site: www.archives.gov," for example, would restrict the results for the phrase "James Brown" to return only pages from the website of the National Archives. You can also use this command to restrict your searches to sites with a specific domain extension—a search for vital records site:.gov will return matches for vital records only on sites in the .gov, or government, domain. Check your favorite search engine's help page to learn what commands are available and become familiar with them.

To eliminate the need to remember all of these search options, you can also use the search engine's advanced search page. Most allow you to use all of the features discussed here by selecting variables from a drop-down list or clicking a check box. Check the search engine's home page for a link to its advanced search.

Get Creative with Names

It's important for genealogists to have an open mind when it comes to names. Your family's surname, for example, was not likely always spelled the same way that it is now. It may have been "Americanized" by your ancestors in order to help them assimilate into their new country and culture. An unusual spelling or non-Latin characters may have begged for simplification. A name change may have also arisen from a desire to conceal nationality or religious orientation for fear of reprisal or discrimination. Or your branch of the family may have just decided to change the spelling to make it easier to spell or because they liked the new name better. Some are simple spelling changes—the German surname Heyer has become Hyer, Hier, Hire, Hires, and Hiers. Other changes are more obscure, such as the surname Toman being "Americanized" to Thomas.

Misspelled names are also extremely common. Most of the records in which you'll find your ancestors were recorded by someone else—a court clerk, a priest, an immigration official—who may not have known how a name was spelled. Your ancestor probably even spelled his own name in different ways at different times. Names are also often just written down wrong, by people who spelled them phonetically, or by individuals trying to transcribe messy handwriting or blurred records for an index.

When searching for your family in online databases, get creative with surname spellings. If your name is plural, such as Owens, search for both Owen and Owens. Use a wildcard in databases that allow it (many genealogy databases do, although Internet search engines generally do not), to help search for several options at once. Examples of this include Owen* to search for Owen or Owens and John* to return surnames such as John, Johnson, Johnsen, Johnathon, and Johns. For each database you search, read the instructions or look for an advanced search page to see what search options are available to you. First names or given names are also candidates for variation. Your Grandmother Elizabeth may also appear in records as Liz, Lizzie, Lisa, Beth, Eliza, Betty, or Bessie. You might also find her listed by her initial, as in E. Martin or E.R. Martin. Some people also go by their middle name; in this case she may be listed as Roberta Martin. These people can sometimes be the most tricky to find, because they'll often choose to use their given name in official records, and use the middle name that they are called in more informal situations. There are families in which all of the children are enumerated in one census by their first names, in the next census by the middle names they more commonly used, and in yet a third census by their initials. The key is to keep an open mind when searching for your ancestors, and to search for all possibilities before you give up.

Critical Clicks
Many genealogy databases offer a search feature called Soundex, a special type of indexing system created for use with the U.S. census and other records, which groups last names based on the way they sound so that similar names will be found together regardless of how they are spelled (e.g., Smith, Smyth, or Smythe). Learn more in the article "Soundex Explained" (*http://genealogy.about.com/od/census/a/soundex.htm*).

Search Tools and Strategies

The hallmark of a good online genealogist is knowing how to work the search engines or databases to find what he seeks. But knowing how to search is not enough, by itself. You also need to know where to search, and what to do with the results. To help you with this, several search tools and strategies are outlined in the following sections.

Bring Back Sites from the Dead

How many times have you found a link to a promising website, only to find that it leads to a File Not Found page? Websites are in a state of constant flux, with webmasters changing file names, switching ISPs, or just taking down the site or letting the domain name lapse because they no longer have the time or interest to maintain it. As frustrating as this is, a File Not Found, or 404 error does not always mean the content is gone forever.

- Trim back the URL. Perhaps someone just moved that particular page into a new folder, or otherwise rearranged or renamed some of the files on the site. Try trimming the URL of the page you're trying to access back to the root domain (the root domain being everything between the http:// and the next backslash) to see if the site exists. If it does, use the "Search" feature or click on likely links or tabs to find the page you want.

- Try Google Cache. When you follow a link from Google that comes up 404, or missing, hit the Back button to return to Google and click on the little cached link at the end of the Google listing for the site. This will bring up a copy of the page as it appeared at the time that Google last indexed the page.
- Visit the Internet Archive. Sometimes sites really are taken offline.

Even that doesn't mean the information is necessarily lost forever. The Wayback Machine at Internet Archive preserves websites for posterity by taking regular "snapshots" of web pages at various points in time. Type a URL into the Wayback Machine search box (*www.archive.org*), then select a date from the available archives and you can begin surfing an archived version of the web page.

Use the Find Feature in Your Browser

Many genealogy transcriptions and records appear online as long scrolling pages of text. To quickly search these pages for a particular name or other piece of information, use the Find feature in your browser. To access the Find feature, press CTRL+F for PCs, or the COMMAND+F for Macs.

Use the Steve Morse One-Step Search tools

The one-step search pages (*www.stevemorse.org*) created by Steve Morse offer enhanced search options for popular genealogical databases such as Ellis Island Records, Ancestry .com, and the Social Security Death Index. In almost every case, the one-step search offers more flexibility than the original database's search engine. Use these one-step tools as a back door when you're unsuccessful at searching popular databases directly.

Find the Right Tree in the Forest

Individuals are unique. Names are not. When searching for your ancestors on the Internet, you'll quickly find that there are numerous people with the same name. Even unusual names may not be as uncommon as you think. Dempsey and Kinchen Owens may sound like unusual names, but there were actually several men sporting those monikers living in mid-nineteenth-century North Carolina!

To avoid the pitfall of merging two people with the same name into one, certified genealogist Marsha Hoffman Rising, author of *The Family Tree Problem Solver*, always assumes that two people of the same name lived in the same community. This reminds you not to attach a piece of data to a specific individual until you're sure that you have the right person. Search for all available records, and use them to identify the distinguishing characteristics of your ancestor. Two men with the same name will have different wives, different children, and perhaps a different occupation. Most important, they won't usually occupy the same piece of property, so be sure to include land and property records in your search.

It's not unusual to find two men of the same name living in the same community identified as "Sr." and "Jr." in local records, causing many researchers to mistakenly connect them as father and son. In reality, they could have a different family relationship, such as uncle and nephew, or even no relationship at all—with "junior" and "senior" used solely to distinguish between an elder and a younger man with the same name. These and other relationship terms such as "aunt" and "cousin" were often used very loosely in earlier times—and still are, even today. The lesson? It's important not to jump to hasty conclusions. Take time to research multiple sources of information for each individual and event in your family tree so you can be sure you have the correct individual identified as your ancestor.

Genealogical Guidance

One popular method for locating ancestors with common surnames such as Smith or Powell is to search for other less-common names from your ancestor's family. If your John Smith has a son named Elias, try searching for Elias Smith. Also look for sisters who married men with more unusual names.

Spread the Wealth

As mentioned in Chapter 1, a "cluster" approach to family history research requires you to branch out your genealogy search to include records of neighbors, family friends, or other individuals with whom your ancestors interacted in some fashion. Certified genealogist Elizabeth Shown Mills memorably refers to this group of individuals as your ancestor's "F.A.N. club" (Friends, Associates, and Neighbors). Cluster genealogy is generally used as a workaround approach when records on your own ancestors are lacking, but some people actually choose to focus their research on a group of unrelated but connected people, such as members of a particular town or school.

In its most simple form, cluster genealogy might mean ordering the death certificate for each of your grandmother's siblings when her death certificate turns up with "unknown" in the blank for mother's maiden name. The hope is that at least one of the siblings' informants knew the mother's maiden name and ensured that it was recorded correctly on their death certificate.

A cluster approach is frequently used to track down the family of a female ancestor. Individuals usually married someone who lived nearby, or was otherwise in the social circle, such as the sibling of a classmate. Expand your research to include the records for individuals named as witnesses on your ancestor's land deeds, or neighbors identified through census or tax lists, and you just might identify your great-great-grandmother's family!

Another, slightly more complex, example of the cluster approach is acquiring copies of and platting the land grants for all of the individuals who owned land in the vicinity of your North Carolina ancestor around 1725, in an effort to distinguish him from another man of the same name who also owned land in the area.

The next time a previously unknown name pops up in a record that relates to your ancestor, spend some time researching him or her. At the very least, be sure to record the name in your research notes in case it pops up again. There may just be a connection there!

CHAPTER 3

Online Starting Points

The Internet is overflowing with tens of thousands of sites with family history information. With just a few clicks of your mouse, you can learn how to get started researching your family history, explore historical databases for your ancestors, share your discoveries with family and friends, and network with other genealogists. It's exciting and addicting, but without a road map, you may quickly find yourself lost.

What Is and Is Not Online

To help acquaint you with genealogy research online, this chapter presents some of the largest and most popular online sites to begin your family history search. Most of these will include sources in the form of the following:

- Indexes—An index is a list of names, possibly including other relevant details such as date or location of an event, that directs you to the original documents in which the names appear.
- Transcriptions and abstracts—In a transcription, the full text of a document is copied out and placed online as text. Sometimes information is "abstracted," which means that only the most relevant details are pulled out.
- Digital images—The original document is scanned and may be presented online as an image file, a PDF file, or a document

that you must view through a special viewer that you'll download to your computer.

Most online data comes in the form of indexes, because they are the least time-consuming and least costly to prepare and place online. This has important implications for genealogists, as it means you cannot do all of your research online. More and more indexes are now being linked to digital scans of the original documents, however. In cases where these scans aren't available online, all information you derive from indexes and transcriptions will have to be checked against the original source—often necessitating a letter, call, or visit to a courthouse, archives, or other records repository.

Explore Free Databases

Thanks to the efforts of hundreds of thousands of volunteer genealogists and historians, there is a wealth of free genealogy data available online. Government agencies, libraries, and archives have also jumped on the digital bandwagon, offering free Internet access to some of the many public records under their domain. Most of these free databases of interest to genealogists will be introduced in the chapters where they are most relevant. The Ellis Island database, for example, will be discussed in Chapter 9. Here, however, you'll learn about some of the largest, general purpose sites for free genealogy research.

Root Around at RootsWeb
The oldest and largest free community genealogy site on the web, RootsWeb (*www.rootsweb.com*), offers hundreds of gigabytes of free genealogy data, including more than 8 million records

contributed by users. Search tabs at the top lead you to some of RootsWeb's most popular features:

- Click on "Searches" to access a variety of search engines and indexes. Here you'll find the RootsWeb Surname List (RSL), a registry of surnames along with information about how to contact the person who submitted the surname so you can share information and compare notes. This is also where you'll find links to the RootsWeb hosted genealogy records and databases, organized by location and/or record type.
- The Family Trees tab takes you to the massive WorldConnect project, a lineage-linked database with more than 600 million names. Learn more about WorldConnect in the "Look in Lineage-Linked Databases" section later in this chapter.
- The next two tabs take you to Mailing Lists and Message Boards, where you can connect with other researchers, ask questions about your family history, or search through more than a decade of archived posts. See Chapter 11 for more on these features.
- RootsWeb also hosts tens of thousands of websites for the genealogy community, including personal sites, surname sites, and major free genealogy projects. The websites tab offers a good jumping-off point for exploring your roots.

Find Local Records at the USGenWeb Project

The goal of this large volunteer genealogy project is to maintain websites for genealogical research in every U.S. state and county. The databases, links, and information found at the USGenWeb Project (*www.usgenweb.org*) are all free, but because the sites are all maintained entirely by volunteers, the quality and quantity of the information vary widely from site to site. Whenever you're researching in a new locality, however, it's a good idea to include a visit to the local GenWeb site to check out the available databases, learn about the area's geography and changing boundaries, and identify local resources for research in the area.

Look in Lineage-Linked Databases

Lineage-linked databases offer family historians an easy way to search, contribute, view, or download family trees online. Instead of just a simple list or index of names, lineage-linked databases present family trees in a linked, pedigree format. Because these compiled databases offer access to millions of names and multiple generations of a family tree, they are a favorite of many online genealogists.

The Internet's largest collection of user-submitted family trees can be found at Ancestry.com, a collection of more than 18 million family trees containing 1.8 billion names, known as Ancestry Member Trees (*http://trees.ancestry.com*).

Another huge collection of family tree files can be found in the combined Ancestry World Tree/RootsWeb WorldConnect database. The database, containing more than one million names in 400+ million family trees, can be searched at both Ancestry.com as Ancestry World Tree (*www.ancestry.com/trees/awt/main.aspx*) or at RootsWeb as RootsWeb WorldConnect (*http://worldconnect.rootsweb.com*). Advanced search options, easy submission of your own family tree, contact information for submitters, and the ability to add electronic notes make this lineage-linked database a favorite with online genealogists.

At FamilySearch.org, the FamilySearch Family Tree (accessible from the Trees tab at *www.familysearch.org*) is another good lineage-linked collection of family trees. It presently includes more than 4.1 billion names drawn from FamilySearch's International Genealogical Index (IGI), Ancestral File (AF), and Pedigree Resource File (PRF). FamilySearch also offers a mobile app that lets you update and manage your family tree on the go.

Despite the convenience of being able to download a big chunk of your family history in one place, lineage-linked or pedigree databases have one huge drawback. They are only as reliable as the researcher or hobbyist who posted them. The first option for evaluating a family tree's reliability is to look for good documentation of sources and conclusions, but to find such well-documented pedigrees online is rare. To ensure that the information you have found is correct, you'll want to follow up all facts in original sources.

Critical Clicks

In addition to the large lineage-linked databases available through Ancestry. com, RootsWeb.com, and FamilySearch, other large pedigree sites (some free and some subscription) include GenCircles (*www.gencircles.com*), GeneaNet (*www.geneanet.org*), Kindred Konnections (*www.mytrees.com*), and OneGreatFamily (*www.onegreatfamily.org*).

Seek Out Subscription Sites

Commercial sites generally offer the greatest wealth of genealogy data, drawn from records around the world. This information comes with a price tag, however, in the form of subscription or pay-per-view access. When evaluating a commercial genealogy site, consider whether the payment is worth the return in terms of the unique databases or records you will gain access to, or the time you will save by being able to access them from your home.

Ancestry.com

The largest commercial online source for family history information, with more than 1.3 million subscribers, is Ancestry .com (*www.ancestry.com*). More than 5 billion digitized historical documents are available to subscribing members from over two-dozen countries, including the United States, Great Britain, and Canada. As a subscriber to Ancestry.com, you can:

- Search for historical records. Ancestry.com has more than 5 billion records available online, including census records, immigration records, historical newspapers, military records, vital records, school yearbooks, and a variety of other resources. Advanced search features allow you to search across all databases at once.
- View digital images of original records. Ancestry.com places a focus on scanning and digitizing historical documents for online viewing. This organization's efforts made it the first site online to offer indexes and images of the complete U.S. census from 1790 to 1930. It also offers digitized passenger lists, British and Canadian census records, the England & Wales National Probate Calendar, a collection of more than 60 million school yearbooks, and U.S. military records such as Civil War pension application cards and WWI draft registration cards.
- Connect with others researching the same ancestors. The large genealogy community at Ancestry.com offers numerous chances to benefit from the research of others. The majority of the community features at Ancestry.com are free and available to even nonsubscribers, including user-submitted family trees and family history message boards.

Ancestry.com is a subscription-based site, offering unlimited access to records for a monthly or annual fee. A special subscription version for libraries, called Ancestry Library Edition, may be available to you for free through your local library, but you'll only have access from the library computers. This database is not available for remote access from home with a library card. Ancestry.com also offers free access to patrons at the Family History Library and select larger Family History Centers, through a special arrangement with the Church of Jesus Christ of Latter-day Saints (the LDS or Mormon Church).

Critical Clicks

Ancestry.com also offers a subscription-based mobile app that will easily help you search for your heritage, whether you're on the couch or on the go. You can use this app to build a family tree, research your family history, and more!

Genealogy Bank

NewsBank offers online access to millions of records from its digital vaults through a service geared specifically to genealogists. Known as GenealogyBank (*www.genealogybank.com*), the subscription-based product, launched in 2006, offers access to more than 480 million articles from more than 4,300 historical U.S. newspapers, plus historical documents and the Social Security Death Index. The biggest draw for genealogists is the historical newspaper collection dating back to 1690, plus the 28 million–plus contemporary obituaries (dating back to 1977). Unlimited access is available for a monthly or annual subscription, and there is a money-back guarantee if you're not satisfied. A similar service called America's GenealogyBank is available for library subscription, so check with your local or state library before you subscribe. You may already have access to this database through one of these sources.

Genealogical Guidance

Digital images of original records found online are considered by most genealogists to offer a reasonable substitute for the original record in almost every research situation. In other words, if you've accessed a digital image of a census enumeration or military record from a reputable source, it's generally not necessary to also view the original record.

Fold3.com

Content at subscription-based Fold3.com (*www.Fold3.com*) is a mix of historical documents and newspapers, with the bulk of the content digitized through a partnership with the National

Archives. Fold3 is best known by genealogists for its U.S. military records collection, including Revolutionary War Pension records, Civil War service records, and Army and Navy JAG Case Files. Other interesting collections among its 67 million–plus images include FBI case files, records of the Southern Claims Commission, U.S. naturalization records, and interactive editions of the 1860 and 1930 U.S. census, which allow users to create profile pages for any enumerated individual.

Fold3 can be searched by name or keyword across all available records, or you can browse or search by collection or historical era. Results can be further narrowed by collection title, category, place, name, and year. The Flash-based site is beautiful and easy to navigate, but searching can be awkward at times. For the best results with more common names, browse directly to the collection/title of interest and then search within that collection. Fold3.com offers both monthly and annual subscription rates, as well as a seven-day free trial.

American Ancestors

The flagship website of the New England Historic Genealogical Society (*www.americanancestors.org*) hosts a large collection of online databases for individuals with New England ancestry, such as Massachusetts vital records and full text issues of the New England Historical and Genealogical Register (from 1847). There is also a growing collection of records for other areas, including resources for mid-Atlantic, Irish, and African American research. Annual membership includes access to more than 3,000 online genealogical and historical collections, plus subscriptions to American Ancestors magazine and The New England Historical and Genealogical Register.

WorldVitalRecords

WorldVitalRecords (*www.worldvitalrecords.com*) offers both free and paid family history content. The company is headed by former MyFamily.com founder Paul Allen. Most of the free content—including the Social Security Death Index, the Bureau of Land Management Records, World War II Army Enlistment Records, and select state death indexes—is also free elsewhere online. Unique content available at WorldVitalRecords includes the SmallTownPapers collection, content from the Everton Genealogical Library, English parish registers, and other genealogical data. WorldVitalRecords stands out for its focus on unusual and less frequently used family history sources from all over the world and its inexpensive subscription price.

Genealogy Today

This relatively inexpensive subscription-based site specializes in unique records of interest for social and family history. Databases available at Genealogy Today (*www.genealogytoday .com*) include school yearbooks, association membership rosters, orphanage records, church records, railroad seniority rosters, farm directories, donation lists, and insurance claims. Most of the information has been transcribed by hand from documents and books found in estate sales, used-book stores, eBay, and so on. The content primarily spans 1830 to 1930 from U.S. sources.

Find Family at FamilySearch

The Family History Library (FHL) in Salt Lake City has the largest collection of genealogical materials in the world, thanks to the diligent work of members of the Church of Jesus Christ of Latter-day Saints. Their online presence at FamilySearch (*www .familysearch.org*) features more than a billion names in search-able databases—all of them free.

Just Enter a Name

A variety of free online databases are available for searching on FamilySearch. You can either just enter a name from the Home Page, or select Show Advanced for additional search fields. Clicking Search will bring up a list of results, along with options on the left-hand side of the screen for narrowing and refining your search results.

- Family Trees (*https://familysearch.org/family-trees*)—Select Trees from the Home Page to bring up a search screen specifically for searching submitted family trees. This large database includes past submissions to the International Genealogical Index (IGI), Ancestral File, and the Pedigree Resource File, plus ongoing lineage-linked family tree submissions submitted by FamilySearch users worldwide.
- Library Catalog (*https://familysearch.org/catalog-search*)—If you're looking to see what records are available at the Family History Library, browse the Library Catalog. See more on this in the next section.
- Historical Records (*www.familysearch.org/search*)—This tab (the main one) includes a search box at the top, plus a list of genealogical records below, organized by country. This is where you'll find the true "meat" of the FamilySearch website, with digitized images and transcribed indexes for millions of family history records from countries all over the world. The biggest focus is on vital record collections, including baptismal records, marriage licenses, death certificates, and even burial records. This collection also includes digitized images and/or transcriptions for the bulk of available federal U.S. census records, plus selected state censuses.

Make Use of the Family History Library Catalog

For a small fee, almost every microfilm in the vast Family History Library collection can be borrowed through your local Family History Center. While you won't be able to borrow or view the films online (at least not yet), you can use the Family History Library Catalog (FHLC) to view available records and plan your research strategy. This virtual catalog to the vast holdings of the Family History Library can be searched by place, surname, title, author, subject, call number, film/fiche number, or keyword. The default Place Search is the most useful search for most genealogy purposes because it will return a list of all available records from the area where your ancestor lived that have been filmed and are available at the Family History Library, along with links if the records have been digitized and are available online.

Borrow Microfilm

Once you find a record of interest in the FHLC, scroll down to the Film Notes to locate call numbers for microfilms that contain the record you seek. With the name of the record and the call number for the film, you can submit a loan request through your local Family History Center. They charge a small fee of a few dollars per microfilm to cover shipping and handling to and from the Family History Library in Salt Lake City. Most films will be available for viewing at your local FHC within a few weeks of your order. Books are generally not available for loan.

Critical Clicks

The LDS Church operates more than 4,000 Family History Centers (FHC) in more than eighty countries around the world. These branch facilities of the Family History Library in Salt Lake City offer access to the library's vast genealogical holdings, through electronic databases and microfilm loan. While these centers are usually located inside buildings belonging to the church, everyone is welcome regardless of their religious beliefs. Visit *www.familysearch.org/centers* to find a Family History Center near you.

Even if you don't plan to borrow microfilms, the FHLC is a great way to view the types of records that are available for your locality and time period of interest. A place search in the catalog for Edgecombe County, North Carolina, for example, displays a wide variety of records, from Bible records to voting registers. By selecting "Court, Land, Wills & Financial" and then "Land Records" from the Category List, you learn that the county maintains deed records from 1732 to 1931, and an index to the deeds from 1759 to 1920.

Access Helpful Research Tools and Guidance

Another thing that FamilySearch does well is teach newcomers about genealogy. Select the Learn section of FamilySearch from the navigation bar at the top of each page to access learning articles in the Research Wiki, Research Forums, and links to online classes from FamilySearch and other providers. From the Learn page, select Browse by Country to learn more about family history research in a particular region, then select your area of interest from the list.

From each Learn page you can access both the FamilySearch Research Wiki and the FamilySearch Research Forums. The Research Wiki (*www.familysearch.org/wiki*) includes FamilySearch research publications such as research outlines and foreign word lists for various countries, states and localities around the world, plus user-submitted advice and content (similar to Wikipedia and other popular Wikis). The Research Forums (*www.familysearch.org/forums*), organized primarily geographically, allow you to search for information, ask questions, or offer answers to others.

Help Index Records

FamilySearch Worldwide Indexing (*www.familysearch.org/indexing*) is a big part of the reason that FamilySearch is able to make so many records available online for free to all researchers.

Tens of thousands of volunteers from all over the world donate their time to help extract data from digitized records using FamilySearch's free online indexing tool. This user-extracted data is then used to create and provide free searchable indexes to digitized historical records on FamilySearch.org. Take the two-minute test drive, accessible from the main Worldwide Indexing page, to see how it works.

Discover History at the National Archives

The U.S. National Archives and Records Administration (NARA) preserves a huge amount of information related to the history of our nation and its people—the paper documents alone would circle the earth more than fifty seven times if laid end to end! Because the records at the National Archives (*www.archives.gov*) come from every branch of the federal government, almost all Americans can find themselves, their ancestors, or their community in the archival holdings.

The cost to digitize such a huge volume of materials is prohibitive, so only a small percentage of the National Archives records are available for research online. Instead, the greatest value of the site is in its research tools, such as microfilm indexes and finding aids, and articles on various record types and how to access them. There are, however, a few exceptions, such as Casualty Lists for the Korean and Vietnam Wars, and Selected Chinese Exclusion Lists. Most of the rest of the available data on its website can be accessed through one of two NARA search engines.

- The Archival Research Catalog (ARC) (*www.archives.gov/research/arc*) is the online catalog of NARA and currently describes about 50 percent of its holdings. In some cases, ARC will take you directly to an online record or database. You can search ARC by keyword, location, organization, person, or topic. You can also restrict your search to return digitized images only, which will include photographs as well as digitized copies of original documents. Useful genealogy databases that can be accessed through ARC include World War II Casualty Lists; indexes to several Native American census rolls, including the Guion-Miller Roll and Dawes Rolls; and fugitive slave case papers and petitions.

- The Access to Archival Databases (AAD) (*http://aad.archives.gov/aad*) allows you to search for free through more than 85 million documents, including passenger lists for people who fled the Irish famine for the United States in the 1840s, photos of natural and manmade disasters, and the popular World War II army enlistment file. Be sure to check out the Search Values feature for any search field you use. In the World War II file, for example, you need to enter names as last name, first name (Owens, James) and the year of birth as a two-digit number (such as 23).

The National Archives has partnered with Fold3.com and Ancestry.com to digitize additional records from its vast holdings, with tens of millions of pages digitized to date. Access to the digitized materials is available for no charge in the National Archives facilities, but the records are only available online at Ancestry.com and/or Fold3.com on a subscription basis. In some cases, the digitized images may be made available at no charge on the National Archives website in the future. National Archives content that is currently available on Fold3 (*www.Fold3.com*) and/or Ancestry (*www.ancestry.com*) is highlighted in this list from the National Archives of "Microfilm Publications and Original Records Digitized by Our Digitization Partners" (*www.archives.gov/digitization/digitized-by-partners.html*).

Look at the Library of Congress

While many may not classify the Library of Congress (*www.loc .gov*) as a starting point for online genealogy research, it has a number of important features and collections that warrant its inclusion in this chapter.

The Library of Congress Online Catalog (*http://catalog.loc.gov*) is one of the best places to search online for published local and family histories. While the books themselves are not available online, you can easily see what books have been published that may relate to your research. With this information you can try contacting local libraries or historical societies to see if they have a copy of this book you can borrow, or have them make copies of the pages that concern your ancestors.

The American Memory Collection (*http://memory.loc.gov*) presents a digital record of American history, chronicling historic events, people, places, and ideas through documents, maps, sheet music, moving images, sound recordings, and oral histories. Enter your family name or hometown in the search box available at the top of each page to see if information about your ancestors or the community in which they lived is included in the online American Memory collection.

Search State Libraries and Archives

The state library or archive can often be a genealogist's best friend—even online genealogists. Many are scanning, digitizing, and indexing the most popular records from their vast holdings, and placing them online for free access by genealogists, historians, and other researchers. Budget shortages and other issues may dictate that new data isn't added as quickly as everyone might like, but these state resources often offer access to databases or indexes not available elsewhere online.

The Illinois State Archives (*www.cyberdriveillinois.com/departments/archives/databases.html*), one of the first to provide online access to selected records, offers a Statewide Marriage Index, 1763 to 1900, and a Statewide Death Index, 1917 to 1950, along with public-domain land sales, emancipation records, military records, and several county-level probate and circuit court indexes. Another good example is the Missouri State Archives (*www.sos.mo.gov/archives/resources/ordb.asp*), where you can search a database of births and deaths prior to 1910, or search and view digital copies of death certificates from 1910 to 1959. They also have indexes and/or abstracts of coroner's inquest records, naturalization records, and pre-1900 St. Louis City and County probate records. For those researching in Virginia, the website of the Library of Virginia (*www.virginiamemory.com/collections*) offers eighty-plus databases, indexes, and finding aids of use to genealogists, including World War I history questionnaires; historical Virginia photographs; and a database of Virginia Land Office patents, grants, and surveys from 1623 to 1992. Try a search for "your state name" archives or "your state name" state library to locate such sites.

CHAPTER 4

Search for Death Records

Since genealogy research begins with the present before moving back into the past, death records are a good place to begin your search. They often provide enough detail to help verify that you have the correct individual, and may include facts that you don't already have to help you reach back to the previous generation. Death records are also among the easiest family history records to find online.

A Good Place to Begin

Why should you care when your grandfather died when what you really want to know is who your great-grandparents were? Death records—including death certificates, tombstone inscriptions, obituaries, and funeral home records—all provide important clues to an individual's past. Your grandfather's death certificate may list the maiden name of his mother, a significant little tidbit that living family members no longer recall. His obituary may mention a surviving sister; the great-aunt that you never knew existed. His tombstone may tell you that he was a member of the Sons of Confederate Veterans. Records from the funeral home may indicate his exact date of birth.

A second, but equally important, reason for beginning a search with death records is that they are among the most easily accessible records. The fact that the individual is deceased makes privacy less of a concern. Now all of this is not to say that you should always begin a genealogy search with death records. There's nothing wrong with beginning with your grandparents' marriage record, or their enumeration in the 1930 U.S. census. But once you've gathered as much information as you can from family members, death records generally make sense as the next good place to take your family history quest.

Search for Obituaries

Whenever you embark on a new family history project, it is often helpful to begin by searching for an obituary. This not only helps confirm the individual's date of death, but often provides extra family details that you may not have—the names of extended family members, place of birth, occupation, religious faith and/ or place of worship, organization memberships, and any other particulars that people felt were important enough to mention in summing up the life of the deceased.

Biographies of soul singer James Brown repeatedly mention his being raised by his Great-Aunt Hansone Washington for a time, but offer few clues as to exactly how she was related. Was she a great-aunt on his mother's side or father's side? Was she an aunt or a great-aunt (the biographies don't agree)? Who were her parents? An online obituary for Mrs. Hansone Washington in the *Augusta Chronicle*, dated Saturday, June 18, 1977, provides some insight:

> Mrs. Hansone Washington, 1029 Bennett Lane died Thursday in an Augusta hospital. Funeral arrangements will be announced by Blount Funeral Home. Survivors include two sisters, Mrs. Josephine Gilliam and Mrs. I. Ganes; two brothers, Mansfield Scott and Willard Scott; and five sons, Stanley E. Figenson, Mike Jowery, Ella Figenson, William Glen, and Johney Washington.

Friends may call at the residence or at Blount Funeral Home.

Armed with the names of her brothers and sisters from this obituary, you can identify the family of Hansone ("Handsome") Scott in the 1910 census of Barnwell County, S.C., prior to her marriage to William Washington and move to Augusta, Georgia. Obituaries for other family members, including the father of James Brown, help clarify her relationship to the singer.

When searching for an obituary, be sure to investigate all likely newspapers. Many cities have more than one paper, and an obituary for a specific individual could appear in more than one town. A thorough search should include the city where the person died and any locations where he or she lived for many years or still have family. You never know which paper is going to have the most detailed obituary, or turn up the one important clue that is omitted from the rest. Check the papers for at least a week after the individual's death. Often a brief obituary or death notice will appear in the first day or two after the death and a longer, full obituary will follow a day or two later.

Obituaries of the past are often not as lengthy and detailed as more modern obituaries. Many of them are little more than a brief notice of the death and funeral arrangements. More recent obituaries are also much easier to locate online, while one from twenty or more years ago may require microfilm research or a request to the newspaper in which it was published. But for a genealogist some information is better than no information at all, so don't assume that obituaries are only useful for people who died within the past few decades.

Look Online

There are many sources for locating obituaries online, such as major historical databases, volunteer obituary transcription sites, and the website of the newspaper itself. Google Archive Search (*http://news.google.com/archivesearch*) provides an easy way to search more than 200 years of archived news content from individual publishers and news aggregators, making it a good place to begin your search. Both free and fee-based content is included in Archive Search. Search results available for a fee are clearly labeled as "pay-per-view" or list a specific fee to access the content. Links from Google take you directly to the website of the publisher or aggregator where the content is hosted. When there are more than just a handful of results, a useful timeline will appear in the left-hand navigation with links to help you drill down into search results by decade or year. None of this is content you can't find through searching directly on the publishers' websites, but Google's service makes it easy to search and navigate through multiple sources at once. If you end up with too many results for the individual's name, try adding search terms such as "obituary," "funeral," or "died" to help focus your results.

A variety of specialized search services can also help you locate an obituary online. The Obituary Daily Times (*www.rootsweb .com/~obituary*) offers a daily index of published obituaries compiled by volunteers and distributed freely via e-mail list. The entire database going back to about 1999 is also searchable online. The Obituary Daily Times does not index all published obituaries, just the ones selected to include by the volunteers. It also does not have the actual newspaper notices, just the name of the deceased, and the publication and date where the obituary appeared. With this information you can then request a copy of the obituary from the library or directly from the newspaper. ObitFinder (*www.obitfinder.com*) from Legacy.com links to online obituaries from U.S. and Canadian newspapers. Some require a fee to access. Obituary Central (*www.obitcentral.com*) organizes links by state and county to transcribed funeral notices and obituaries appearing on various genealogy websites going back to about 1998. It also links directly to search results for death notices on newspaper websites.

Subscription-based obituary and newspaper search sites such as ObitsArchive.com, NewspaperARCHIVE.com, and the National Obituary Archive (*www.arrangeonline.com/obituary*) can also be useful in locating obituaries. Many general genealogy subscription sites also get into the act; Ancestry.com, Fold3.com, and World Vital Records (*www.worldvitalrecords.com*), for example, all offer online obituary and/or historic newspaper collections.

Critical Clicks

Searches for obituaries in Google Archive Search often yield results from the NewsBank service with a per-article access fee that varies by publisher. If you think you'll need to look at more than one or two articles or obituaries, you may get a better value through GenealogyBank (*www.genealogybank.com*). Their America's Obituaries collection contains more than 28 million obituaries from NewsBank, dating from 1977 to the present.

Locate Newspaper Websites

Use your favorite search engine to locate newspapers published in the area where your ancestor lived or died. A search for the town or county name and newspaper will usually turn up what you need. If you know the newspaper's title, you can search for that directly. Once you find the newspaper's website, visit the Obituaries section to see how far back in time these go. Look for an Archives section as well, where the newspaper offers access to older material. Some newspapers leave obituaries online forever, some for a year, some for just a week or two. Some may charge for access to older articles and obituaries.

Look for a Library Website

The public library that serves the area in which your ancestor lived or died is often an excellent source for obituary and death notices. Many maintain obituary clipping files or, at the very least, have back issues of area newspapers available on microfilm. Many library websites even offer online indexes to obituary notices from their area. From there it often takes no more than an e-mail or quick letter to get a copy of the actual obituary; some librarians will even e-mail a digitized copy of the obituary. Many libraries don't charge for this service or request only minimal reimbursement for copying and postage. If you can't find anything on the website, contact the library via phone or e-mail to see how its staff handles such requests. See Chapter 7 for more about locating and using libraries in your genealogy research.

Utilize Your Local Library

Many libraries subscribe to a variety of helpful research databases for free use by their patrons. Subscriptions to databases such as NewsBank, America's GenealogyBank, ProQuest Obituaries, or Ancestry Library Edition can be useful for obituary searches. Contact your local or state library to see what databases are offered (most list them on their website) and whether you can connect from home with your library card number.

Social Security Death Index

When you're unsure of an individual's date of death, head straight for the Social Security Death Index (SSDI). This large database compiled by the U.S. Social Security Administration (SSA) contains vital information for more than 87 million people (primarily Americans) whose deaths have been reported to the SSA.

What You Will Find in the SSDI

Once you locate an individual in the Social Security Death Index, you may find some or all of the following information:

first and last name, date of death, date of birth, social security number (SSN), the state where the SSN was issued, the last known residence of the deceased, and the location where the last SSA benefit was sent.

What You Won't Find in the SSDI

The biggest mistake that researchers make when using the SSDI is in assuming that it is an index to all deceased individuals who have held social security numbers. That is not the case. It is also not a database of all deceased who have received social security benefits, or whose families have received survivor benefits. Instead the SSDI indexes individuals whose deaths were reported to the Social Security Administration, the majority of them after 1962 when SSA first computerized the processing of benefits. If a relative of the deceased or the funeral director did not report the death, or if the individual died prior to 1963, you probably won't find that person's name in the index.

How to Search the SSDI

The complete Social Security Death Index, current up to within the past few months, is available for free searching online on several different websites. A few sites require a fee for access, but their offerings are no better than the free versions. A good place to start is the handy search form by Steve Morse titled "Searching the Social Security Death Index in One Step" (*www.stevemorse .org/ssdi/ssdi.html*). It combines all of the desirable search features from the various SSDI websites into one easy search. Other free SSDI search options include RootsWeb (*http://ssdi.rootsweb .com*) and American Ancestors (*www.americanancestors.org/home .html*—look under "Free Databases").

Locating a particular individual in the large SSDI database, especially if you aren't sure when and where this person died, can be an exercise in frustration. Be sure to take advantage of all the search features available to you, and try different combinations of searches.

- Search by last name or first name only, in combination with other known facts such as date or year of birth and state of last residence. The first name in combination with the exact birth date, or month and year of birth, often produces results.
- Search for women under both their married name and their maiden name.
- Enter an initial in the given name field.
- Omit the zip code because this field does not exist for earlier records.
- Try alternate spellings in the name field, making use of wild-card operators when available.

Order a Copy of the Social Security Application

With the name and social security number from the SSDI, you can request a copy of your ancestor's original application for social security, otherwise known as Form SS-5. This form was completed by individuals applying for a social security number and asked for information that is of great value to genealogists, such as parents' names (including the mother's maiden name), date of birth, employer, and, later, the place of birth. The fee to receive the Social Security Application Form is a bit steep, but well worth it if you don't already know the information that the form often provides.

The Social Security Administration offers online ordering of photocopies of Social Security Number Application SS-5 forms. A link to the application form with current fees can be found in their Guide to Freedom of Information Act (FOIA) requests (*www.ssa.gov/foia*).

Death Certificates and Online Indexes

A death certificate can provide important facts about a person's life—date and cause of death, date and place of birth, parents' names (including mother's maiden name), funeral home, burial location, and name of the informant who provided the information. Since about 1967, most death certificates in the United States also list the deceased's social security number. Actual details included on a death certificate vary from state to state and by time period.

Death certificates in the United States are primarily a twentieth-century innovation. Most states did not officially register deaths until after 1900; some, such as Georgia and New Mexico, began as late as 1919! There are a few exceptions, namely in New York, New Jersey, and the New England states, where recording of deaths began in the mid to late 1800s. In the United States, death certificates are generally maintained at the state level, usually through the Department of Health or Vital Records.

Privacy laws may restrict access to death certificates for a certain period of time after the individual's death. A term of fifty years is fairly common. Some agencies will allow anyone to request a copy of a death certificate, but will black out certain more private information such as the cause of death or social security number unless you are a direct relative of the deceased. When requesting a death certificate from a vital records agency, be prepared to identify your relationship with the deceased and to provide a copy of a valid ID.

Death indexes are available online for many states, counties, and locations. Check first on the website of the state vital records office, state archives, and state library. The Ohio Historical Society, for example, includes an online Ohio Death Certificate Index, 1913 to 1944. The Illinois State Archives hosts the Illinois

Statewide Death Index, 1913 to 1950. At the Minnesota State Archives website you can search an index for death certificates from 1908 to 2001. Genealogist Joe Beine organizes links to these and many other online death indexes at Online Searchable Death Indexes and Records (*www.deathindexes.com*).

The Historical Records collection at FamilySearch (*https:// familysearch.org/search*) offers the largest free online collection of death indexes and certificates, for the United States as well as for many other countries around the globe. Ancestry.com offers access to a wide variety of death indexes to its subscribers. Some of these are also available elsewhere on the web, and some are exclusive online to Ancestry.com. Death indexes can also be found on a variety of other genealogy sites, both free and fee-based. The state and county sites at USGenWeb (*www.usgenweb.org*) are a good place to find death record transcriptions and indexes, as well as links to offsite indexes. Genealogical society websites are another good place to try. Both the Italian Genealogical Group (*www.italiangen.org*) and German Genealogy Group (*www .germangenealogygroup.com*), for example, offer online searching of the New York City Death Index, 1862 to 1948. When all else fails, try a search for "death index" and the state name, such as Pennsylvania "death index," in your favorite search engine.

Critical Clicks

Vitalrec.com (*www.vitalrec.com*) offers current information for each U.S. state on the availability of death records, instructions and fees for ordering a death certificate copy, and a link to the state department that handles vital records. If you're in a hurry, VitalChek (*www.vitalchek.com*) processes online rush orders for each state, including online credit card payment—for an extra fee, of course.

One last important online source for death information is the International Genealogical Index (IGI) at FamilySearch (*www.familysearch.org*). This free database contains millions of birth, marriage, and death dates and places for deceased people from countries around the world, drawn both from extracted vital records and information supplied by members of the LDS Church. Remember to check the source information to see where the dates you've found were obtained, and verify them with other sources whenever possible.

Visit Virtual Cemeteries and Funeral Homes

Cemetery tombstones or grave markers are good sources for death information, as well as providing evidence for date of birth, family relationships, military service, and membership in fraternal organizations or societies. A visit to the cemetery is a must for family tree projects, but not always easily done in person. While it can't quite match the special feeling you get standing before your ancestor's tombstone, online research in the form of tombstone transcriptions and photographs affords the opportunity for "virtually" traipsing through cemeteries around the world from the comfort of home.

Tombstones often show the age of the individual when she died in place of either the date of birth or death. If this information is provided in the form of years, months, and days, such as "Age 22 Years 11 Months and 26 Days," then you can easily calculate the missing date with the help of a birth date calculator (just type "birth date calculator" into your favorite search engine).

Virtual Cemeteries Have Their Shortcomings

Convenient as it is to research cemetery records online, there are a few disadvantages over a firsthand visit to the cemetery. Keep these in mind as you explore cemetery information online:

- Tombstone information may not always be read and transcribed correctly. Some grave markers can be very hard to read, or the transcriber may have mistyped the information when putting it online. He may also have missed information inscribed on the back of the stone (although the thorough ones won't).

• The arrangement of graves in the cemetery can be important because family members are often buried together or close to one another. That arrangement is not always preserved in the alphabetical listings you sometimes find online. Check to see if some type of placement information has also been transcribed, such as the cemetery section and row. This can at least help identify people buried in the same general area of the cemetery. If the site also includes individual tombstone photos, you can sometimes find clues in them to help identify a gravestone's relative position in the cemetery.

Find Online Cemetery Databases and Lists

Genealogical societies and volunteers are the greatest source for online cemetery transcriptions, so a good place to begin is on the website of an area genealogical society or the appropriate county site at USGenWeb. If that doesn't pan out, use a search engine to locate online cemeteries or transcriptions by entering a phrase such as "Greene County Virginia Cemetery." Or visit ePodunk (*www.epodunk.com*) or the Geographic Names Information System (*http://geonames.usgs.gov*) to find the names of cemeteries in a given town or county and then search for the cemeteries directly by name. These sites won't usually pick up small family cemeteries, but they at least offer a place to start.

Genealogical Guidance
The symbols and architecture you encounter in the cemetery can tell you a lot about your ancestors. *Stories in Stone* by Douglas Keister details many examples of funerary architecture and tombstone symbols, accompanied by photos. Alternatively, look online for information by searching for phrases such as "tombstone symbols" or "cemetery symbolism."

In an effort to preserve the valuable information crumbling away in cemeteries, and to improve access to this information for genealogists, a variety of groups and organizations are collaborating to put cemetery data online. Best of all, these databases are all free!

- Find a Grave—Visit the well-organized Find a Grave site (*www .findagrave.com*) to search more than 49 million grave records for both the famous and the unknown.
- Interment.net—Almost 4 million cemetery records are available for searching or browsing on Interment.net (*www.interment.net*), representing more than 8,000 cemeteries around the world.
- USGenWeb Tombstone Transcription Project—Browse by state and county to view hundreds of thousands of cemetery transcriptions and photos contributed by volunteers to this special project at USGenWeb (*www.usgwtombstones.org*).
- JewishGen Online Worldwide Burial Registry—Well over 1.3 million names are available for searching in this database of Jewish interments in cemeteries and other burial sites world-wide (*www.jewishgen.org/databases/cemetery*).
- Veterans Affairs Nationwide Gravesite Locator—Search for burial locations of veterans with the help of the U.S. Department of Veterans Affairs (*http://gravelocator.cem.va.gov*). The site includes information on veterans and their family members buried in veterans and military cemeteries, as well as those buried in private cemeteries where the grave is marked with a government grave marker.

Don't Disregard Funeral Home Records

Genealogists often overlook the records maintained by funeral homes. These can be a very valuable source of family history information. Depending on state or local laws, the funeral director may be the one responsible for filing the death certificate and placing the obituary with the news media, which means all of those valuable details collected from family members may reside in his files. A funeral home file may provide the deceased's date and place of birth, maiden name if a female, date and place of death, burial location, parents' names, veteran status, social security number and, sometimes, names of surviving relatives.

It is important to realize, however, that a funeral home is a private business. Its primary responsibility is to the deceased and the grieving family, not to genealogists. You may find the funeral home to be reluctant about releasing private records. You may also find that older records are stored away in boxes in a basement or attic, or have been thrown out to make room for more current records.

Some funeral home records may be found online in the form of transcribed data. These records are generally posted by genealogical societies or volunteers; not the funeral homes. There are exceptions, however. The records of the J.F. Bell Funeral Home in Charlottesville prior to 1970 have been placed online (*www .virginia.edu/woodson/projects/bell/intro.html*) in a collaboration between the funeral home and the African American Genealogy Group of Charlottesville. To find funeral home records in your area of interest, do a search for funeral records and the location you are searching—for example, "funeral records Missouri." You can also use the Internet to locate funeral homes in the area in which you're researching, using an online funeral home directory such as FuneralNet (*www.funeralnet.com*).

If you're unable to find any funeral home records online, you may wish to contact the funeral home directly. For best results, address a written request to the manager of the funeral home. This gives him the opportunity to respond at his convenience. Be specific about what you're looking for, enclose a self-addressed stamped envelope, and offer to pay for any copying expenses.

CHAPTER 5

Check the Census

Most people are familiar with the U.S. census, but did you know that federal census takers have been going door-to-door asking questions of American families since 1790? Although it is instituted and maintained primarily to track the nation's population for government planning, a census is among the records that genealogists refer to most frequently because it captures detailed information on an individual or family at a particular point in history—essentially a once-per-decade snapshot of the country's inhabitants. Begin with Grandpa or Great-Grandma in the 1930 census, and you may be able to use the clues you find there to march your family all the way back through census records to 1850!

The U.S. Federal Census

Census records are an important tool for family history research. From them, you can learn who was living in a household at a given point in time, including spouses, siblings, and possibly even a mother-in-law. Census records can also tell you the approximate age of the individuals, where they were born, and what they did for a living. Some census records also provide detail on an individual's immigrant status, including the year of immigration and whether the immigrant applied for U.S. citizenship. Best of all, every available U.S. federal census from 1790 to 1930 can be accessed online.

The first federal census, instituted by President George Washington in 1790, was intended to provide information on residents for the purpose of apportioning members of the House of Representatives and assessing federal tax. Since that first census, the U.S. government has conducted a federal census, or decennial census, once every ten years. However, data from more recent censuses are not available for public inspection because of a seventy-two-year restriction imposed by law to protect the privacy of living individuals. This means the most recent census currently open for public access is 1930 (the 1940 census was released to the public and is available online as of April 1, 2012).

Before 1850, census schedules recorded only the name of the head of household and numbers and approximate ages of any other people living in the home. As the country's population grew, the government's need for additional information also grew and new questions were added to the census. The 1850 census is an important census document for researchers, as it was the first census to list names and ages for all individuals in a household, as well as including the place of birth. Another key year is 1880, as it marked the first federal census to document the relationship of household members to the head of household.

In 1900, the census asked for the month as well as year of birth, providing more detailed information on ages than any census before or since. It is also the first available census record to document immigration and citizenship data, asking whether an individual was foreign born, the year of immigration, the number of years in the United States, and the citizenship status of foreign-born individuals over the age of twenty-one. As the twentieth century progressed, additional questions were added to each census, while others were dropped. Most notable: the 1910 census recorded survivors of the Union or Confederate Army or Navy, the 1920 census asked for the year of naturalization for naturalized citizens, and the 1930 census recorded whether the family owned a radio set.

Critical Clicks

Census extraction forms offer a convenient method for extracting and recording the information that you find as you explore online census records, making it easy to see at a glance what information was collected for a specific census year. Download them for free online from sites such as Ancestry.com (*www.ancestry.com/download/forms#uscensus*), About .com Genealogy (*http://genealogy.about.com/od/free_charts/a/us_census .htm*), and CensusTools (*www.censustools.com*).

What the Census Can Tell You about Your Ancestors

While the early censuses were little more than a head count of the population, more modern census records are filled with a wealth of valuable data. Most significantly, the 1850 to 1930 censuses can provide such details as:

- Names of family members
- Ages for each individual
- State or country of birth
- Parents' birthplaces
- Street address
- Estimated value of their home and personal belongings
- Marriage status and years of marriage
- Occupation
- When they came to the United States and from which country (if applicable)

What you can gain from census records is a wonderful snapshot in time for a particular family or place. You can learn whether your ancestors were literate or spoke English and where they and their parents came from, and even discover neighbors and nearby relatives. By locating your ancestors in multiple census years, you can watch the family grow, and the children move out and start families of their own. You can even use census records to discover whether your ancestors moved, changed jobs, or lost a child.

Access Census Images and Indexes Online

Traditionally, utilizing census records to research your family tree has involved wading through microfilm copies of the original handwritten pages, produced by the U.S. government to preserve the records from decay. These microfilmed census records are generally available for viewing at Family History Centers, the National Archives, and libraries with large genealogy or local history sections.

Because census lists were typically recorded in order of visitation, searching for a particular family on a microfilmed record can be cumbersome and time-consuming. The U.S. government did create indexes for many census years to assist researchers in locating specific individuals or families in the microfilmed census records; however, not all census records were indexed, and most were indexed only by the head of household—the individual identified to the census taker as the person responsible for the care of the home and/or family. With the recent advent of every-name computerized indexes, however, knowing the name of your ancestor or relative and the state he or she resided in is often enough to take you directly to the exact page and line where your ancestor is recorded.

Digitized images of original census pages are now readily available online, and every-name indexes allow you to click directly from your search results to a digital copy of the original census page where your ancestors were recorded—in the enumerator's own handwriting. Digital images are the best census records available online because they allow you to look directly at the record as it was originally created, without having to worry about whether a modern-day transcriber misread the handwriting or mistyped the data. Digital images also allow you to look at all of the information included on the original census, while transcriptions usually only include some of the most important details.

> **Critical Clicks**
> Free trials, available from most subscription genealogy sites, offer a great way to "try before you buy." Such trial periods are generally short, so make the most of your time by creating a list of the people and records you want to search before you sign up. This will help you better evaluate whether to continue or cancel the subscription.

This is where Internet genealogy research really provides a boost over more traditional microfilm research. The entire U.S. census, including complete every-name indexes and digital images of the microfilmed pages, is available for searching and viewing on the Internet. The most comprehensive collection of U.S. census records is available through a subscription to Ancestry.com, which offers the only complete set of digitized images for the entire available U.S. census (1850–1930), as well as every-name indexes for each year. The largest census collections available online include:

- Ancestry.com—All available census images and indexes (Fee-based for individual subscribers; free at subscribing libraries)
- HeritageQuest—Complete set of census images, but not all are indexed (Free; available only at participating libraries)
- FamilySearch.org—Every-name indexes for all census years (1850–1920 with 1930 in progress) and digital images for some years (Free, online)
- Fold3.com—1860 and 1930 complete, with other years being added (Fee-based, online)

Census indexes and images are also available online for other countries, including Canada, England, Scotland, Wales, Ireland, and France.

Check Census Gateway Sites

Census indexes, transcriptions, and abstracts that have been placed online by volunteers and organizations can be most easily found by using a census directory site such as Census Online (*www.census-online.com*). This gateway site has organized links to thousands of free census records from the United States and Canada. Just click on your state of interest, then choose a county to view a list of census records from that area that have been transcribed or digitized. Links to census records at fee-based sites such as Ancestry.com are also included, but are separated from the free links at the bottom of the page and are clearly marked.

Other good census directories for locating free online census records include:

- Census Finder (*www.censusfinder.com*)
- African American Census Schedules Online (*www.afrigeneas .com/aacensus*)

Search or Browse the USGenWeb Census Project

Two large volunteer census efforts, both using the USGenWeb name, are outgrowths of the official USGenWeb Project. Neither is formally affiliated with the USGenWeb any longer, although they both still bear its name. Both census projects, however, still display the same volunteer spirit, offering free access to U.S. census data transcribed and put online by volunteers.

The first USGenWeb Census Project (*www.us-census .org*) is hosted online by USGenNet. The navigation is very straightforward, making it easy to see at a glance what census records are available. Select On-Line Census Inventory to view available census records organized by state, then county. Then use your browser's Find feature to search the page for your names of interest. In some cases a link to a scanned census image is also available. Alternatively, you can use the site's search engine to search across all census records.

The second USGenWeb Census Project (*www.usgwcensus.org*) also offers straightforward navigation. Select a state from the right-hand column to view available census transcriptions. The data is displayed in a uniform text format, which can be easily searched by using your browser's Find feature. This site does not link transcriptions to census images.

Which census year should I search first?

It's generally a good idea to begin with the most current census year available and work backward. In most cases, this is the 1940 census. If your ancestor was deceased by 1940, begin your search with the most recent census taken while he was still living, or the most recent census for which you know his location.

Access Census Records Online Through Your Local Library

Your library card could be your key to free census access. Hundreds of state, county, and local libraries offer free access to U.S. federal census indexes and images through subscriptions to Ancestry Library Edition or HeritageQuest Online. In the case of HeritageQuest Online, you can even save yourself a trip to the library and access the database remotely from home by logging in with your library card number (sometimes this requires signing up with your library first). Ask your local or state library whether they subscribe to these databases, or check out this fairly comprehensive list (from Dick Eastman) of libraries offering remote access to HeritageQuest Online (*www.eogen .com/HeritageQuestOnline*).

Census Research Tips and Caveats

Census enumerations are by no means the most reliable of records. At the time the census was recorded, the enumerator may have missed someone, written a name down wrong, or received inaccurate information. It's not uncommon to find someone who has aged less than five years in the decade between censuses, or whose birthplace changed with each successive decade. Throw in bad handwriting, changing county borders, and missing or illegible records, and there are plenty of opportunities for research frustration.

Because genealogists researching online typically use indexes to locate people in the census, there also exists the extra challenge of dealing with the misinterpretations, typographical errors, and other inaccuracies that often creep in during the census indexing process. This second opportunity for error means that a name could actually have been butchered twice. Perhaps the census taker, tired at the end of a long, hot day, didn't take the time to ask Robert Stuart how his name was spelled, and recorded Stewart instead of Stuart. The individual later responsible for indexing the data was unable to accurately decipher the sloppy handwriting of that tired census taker and interpreted Stewart as Steward. Now, Robert Stuart is Robert Steward and much more difficult to find.

Don't let these caveats scare you away from census records. Census data provides a valuable look at your ancestors in a particular place and time. Census records are also easy to find and use, and can yield a lot of information in a little time. Just keep in mind that census records and indexes are prone to inaccuracy, and the clues found within should always be corroborated with other records when possible.

Be Creative . . . and Patient

When you're having trouble finding your ancestor in the census index, it's time to get creative. Her name may have been misspelled in the census enumeration, or misread when it was indexed. Think about how the name might look instead of how it should look, considering some of the following suggestions:

- Try alternate spellings for both the first name and last name.
- Search with just a first name and location.
- Don't count solely on Soundex; it doesn't pick up all spelling options for a surname.
- Try a nickname and/or middle name in the first name field.
- Substitute an initial for the first name.
- Search for other family members or even neighbors when you can't find your ancestor.

Genealogical Guidance

Old handwriting is often a challenge to read, so it's no wonder census indexes are prone to inaccuracies. The surname CARTER, for example, might have been read as GARTER, or the name CRISP might be spelled as CHRISP or CRIPS. Create a list of alternative spellings for your ancestor's surnames and then try these name variations in every database you search.

Expect Little from the 1890 Federal Census

More than 99 percent of the 1890 census population schedules were damaged in a fire, and their remains later destroyed by government order. The few fragments that survive include only about 6,000 names out of an original count of more than 62 million. Although most census sites allow you to search the 1890 census, and some have beefed up those names with alternative records from the time period, your chances of finding the person you're looking for are slim.

Explore the Community

A census enumeration is much more than a record of an individual family. It also tells the story of an entire community. After you get over the excitement of discovering your ancestor, take time to become familiar with the people living nearby. Neighbors could turn out to be related, even if they don't share the same name. It's not uncommon to find a wife's parents living nearby, or an uncle, or married sister. This is especially true in more rural communities. Becoming familiar with the neighbors also allows you to use their names as a search tool to help locate your ancestor in other census records. For best results, look at several households, if not several pages, on either side of your ancestor and add their names to your research log as well.

Pay Attention to Penmanship

While you're exploring the community, it is also useful to spend time familiarizing yourself with the enumerator's handwriting. Each census taker will have a particular way of styling certain letters, such as a, f, h, j, p, and s. Scan the pages on either side of your ancestor for easily recognizable names to learn how the enumerator wrote certain letters and letter combinations. This will help you to better judge the spelling of your own ancestor's name, as well as those of his family members.

Go to the Original Record When Possible

Census indexes and transcriptions can provide the information many genealogists want most to find—names, dates, and locations. The original census record, however, will almost always include more. By checking the original census image, you will often discover information that may have been misread or was left out of the transcription. And yes, digitized census images are generally considered an acceptable alternative to the original record.

Follow Census Clues to New Records

Census enumerations are packed with details, both large and small. Once you get past the names, ages, and relationships of the listed individuals, there are still many other clues to be found hidden among the census columns. Everything from the street address to the age of a mother at the time of her first marriage may hold a clue that leads to new records. Generally, you should look at every single piece of information contained in a census record (or any record for that matter) and ask yourself what it tells you about your ancestor. Does it fit what you know about him or her? If there is an anomaly, follow it up. It may be an error introduced during the census enumeration process, or it may just be the key to learning something new.

Many, many clues can be gleaned from a census record if you take enough time to fully explore the data recorded in each column, and compare the answers from one census to the next. To get you started, here are a few of the more obvious items to investigate in U.S. federal census records.

Number of Children

Column 11 of the 1900 census and Column 11 of the 1910 census asked for "mother of how many children." When combined with the "number of children living" indicated in the next column, much can be learned. First compare the number of living children with the number of children listed in the household. Do they match up? If not, this may indicate children who were old enough to move out on their own (married or not), or were living elsewhere, such as in an institution, as an apprentice to another family, or with relatives. If there are more children listed in the household than born to the mother, this could possibly indicate a prior marriage of the father. Go back to previous census years to see if you can identify these children and then search for them again in 1900 or 1910 to learn where they are living.

A discrepancy between the number of children born and the number still living obviously indicates that one or more children have probably died. Again, go back to prior census years to identify as many children as possible and, hopefully, determine which ones are deceased prior to 1900 or 1910. Follow up with a search for death certificates, obituaries, and so on.

Marriage Age and Year

The 1910 and 1920 U.S. federal census both contain a column for "number of years in present marriage." Some simple subtraction gives you an approximate date of marriage—something easy to follow up in marriage records.

For ancestors who lived in 1930, pay special attention to Column 15, which asks for "age at first marriage." For married couples, compare that age with their "age at last birthday" from Column 13 to determine the approximate year that each was married. In many cases, it will be the same, give or take a year or two, as you might expect for a married couple. But if this subtraction indicates that the husband was first married eighteen years ago and the wife only eight years ago, there is likely at least one other marriage in the picture. On the other hand, it could just be a recording error on the part of the census enumerator.

Year of Immigration and Naturalization

The 1900, 1910, 1920, and 1930 censuses each include a column that asked for the individual's year of immigration, which can obviously help narrow the timeframe for passenger arrival manifests. It's not uncommon to find a wife immigrating a few years after her husband, as he came ahead to pave the way for his family. In the case of married couples, compare the year of immigration for both spouses with the date of marriage (actual or approximate) to learn if the couple was likely married before or after their arrival in the United States, which in turn narrows the search grid for the wife's parents.

Military Service

The 1910 census includes a column (30) to record whether the person was a "survivor of the Union or Confederate Army or Navy," indicated by "UA" for Union Army, "UN" for Union Navy, "CA" for Confederate Army, and "CN" for Confederate Navy. The 1930 census (Column 31) also asks about military service. A "CW" in this column indicates a Civil War veteran, "Sp" for Spanish-American War, "Phil" for Philippine Insurrection, "Box" for Boxer Rebellion, "Mex" for Mexican Expedition, and "WW" for World War I. Follow up these individuals in military service and pension records.

Street Address

Running vertically down the left-hand side of the 1880 and 1900 through 1930 censuses, you may find a street name indicated. This will vary depending on whether your ancestor lived in a city/town, or a more rural area. Sometimes streets were just not recorded. If they were, however, the first column to the right of the street name includes the house number. With this information you can locate your ancestor in city directories or place their house on a historical or present-day map. The map can be used to place their neighbors as well, including those who lived behind them or across the street, as well as next door.

Special and State Censuses

Special non-population schedules, which include agricultural, manufacturing, and mortality schedules, can be an untapped gold mine for genealogists, providing information on recently deceased individuals and little details of an ancestor's occupation. Other special censuses enumerated slaves, military veterans and their widows, Native Americans, and even deaf couples. A number of states and localities conducted censuses as well, often during the intervening years between federal census schedules. These are all records you may wish to explore once you've been through the federal census records.

> **Critical Clicks**
> A special interim census, partially funded by the federal government, was conducted in 1885 by the states of Colorado, Florida, Nebraska, and the territories of Dakota and New Mexico. These special state and territorial censuses are available online for subscribers of Ancestry .com. The Florida State Census of 1885 is also available online for free at FamilySearch.org.

Slave Schedules (1850–1860)

Slaves were enumerated separately during the 1850 and 1860 census. These slave schedules generally don't list slaves by name, however, instead distinguishing them only by age, sex, color, and the name of the slave owner. A free index and images to the 1850 U.S. Census slave schedules is available online at FamilySearch .org. Ancestry.com includes images and indexes for the 1850 and 1860 slave schedules.

Mortality Schedules (1850–1885)

Mortality schedules were prepared in conjunction with the regular population census to record information about deaths that had occurred in the year prior to the census, including name, age, sex, color, marital status, birthplace, occupation, month of death, and cause of death. These mortality schedules survive for the years 1850 through 1880, as well as for the special federal census of 1885 for Colorado, Florida, Nebraska, New Mexico, and North and South Dakota. Mortality schedules are available by subscription on Ancestry.com. FamilySearch.org offers free access to the 1850 Mortality Schedule.

Agricultural Schedules (1850–1880)

Farmers that produced an excess of $100 worth of products (up to $500 worth on farms larger than three acres by 1870) were asked to provide information on their farm, crops, and livestock. If your ancestor was listed as a farmer on the 1850, 1860, 1870, or 1880 population census, you can find these schedules online at Ancestry.com.

Manufacturing and Industry Schedules (1820, 1850–1880)

Manufacturing, mining, fishing, commercial, and trading businesses that produced more than $500 worth of goods or services were asked to report on the type and operation of their business, with questions covering everything from the kinds and quantities of raw materials used, to the number of women and men employed in their operation. Many of these schedules are available online at Ancestry.com. You should especially follow up on these if your ancestor was listed in the population schedule with a manufacturing type of occupation such as flour miller or candle maker.

Veterans Schedules (1840 and 1890)

Living Revolutionary War pensioners were recorded on the back of the regular 1840 U.S. population schedules. In 1890, a special census was conducted for veterans of the Union Army and their widows. As with the rest of the 1890 census, only a portion of these special Civil War veterans' schedules has survived. The 1840 Census of Pensioners is available online here: *www .newhorizonsgenealogicalservices.com/1840-census-of-pensioners.htm*.

The surviving 1890 veterans schedules are available online at Ancestry.com.

Defective, Dependent, and Delinquent (DDD) Schedules

The 1880 Federal Census included seven supplemental schedules that collected additional information on household members identified as belonging to one of the following classes: insane, idiots, deaf mutes, blind, paupers and indigent persons, homeless children, and prisoners. Ancestry.com has these 1880 DDD schedules online for several, but not all states. You can also access a Special Census on Deaf Family Marriages and Hearing Relatives from 1888–1895 at Ancestry.com, which includes information drawn from questionnaires distributed to deaf couples as well as their hearing relatives as part of a research study conducted on the marriages of the deaf in America by the Volta Bureau in Washington, D.C.

Utilize Census Alternatives

City and county directories, as well as tax rolls, serve as an excellent resource in conjunction with or as an alternative to census records. Since they document at least some of the inhabitants of an area at a given point in time, both can be useful in cases where census records no longer exist, or when you've "misplaced" an ancestor between the decennial censuses.

Tax Lists

Early tax lists generally include all white males over the age of twenty-one, and indicate whether they owned land, slaves, or other taxable property. They usually do not include any other personal information. A Google search for "tax lists genealogy" brings up a wide variety of tax lists online, including 1790/1800 Virginia Tax Lists (*www.binnsgenealogy.com/VirginiaTaxListCensuses*) and Eighteenth Century Tax Lists of Perquimans County, North Carolina (*http://perqtax.homestead.com*).

City Directories

City directories are much like phone directories, a listing of an area's residents. They differ, however, in that they predate the invention of the telephone and often provide additional information about the listed individuals, such as the street address, place of employment, occupation, or name of spouse. Some also offer a separate street directory, sometimes referred to as a crisscross or reverse directory. This makes it easier to find neighbors, as well as nearby churches, cemeteries, and schools. City directories are compiled through door-to-door surveys and published at irregular intervals. Because they are published based on sales value, they are generally available only for large cities and communities.

City or county directories are especially useful for tracking families between census years, for locating an individual's place of business, and for learning the layout of the area in which your ancestors lived. They aren't always easy to find, however. The Library of Congress (*www.loc.gov/rr/microform/uscity*) has a large collection of U.S. city directories available on microfilm. While they are not available for online perusal or through interlibrary loan, the list of available directories can be browsed for clues to cities and years in which city directories were published. City Directories of the United States of America (*www.uscitydirectories .com*) presents an organized directory of links to city directories that have been microfilmed along with the repositories where the microfilm copies can be accessed. It also includes links to city directory transcriptions that have been made available online. Ancestry.com offers indexes and browsable images of more than 10,000 city directories from cities and states across the United States in its U.S. City Directories collection (*http://search.ancestry .com/search/db.aspx?dbid=1540*), covering the years 1820 through 1960. Fold3.com also has a number of early twentieth and late nineteenth-century city directories in its online collection.

CHAPTER 6

Find Family Connections

Marriage records are something a genealogist always hopes to find because they help to "tie the knot" between two branches of the family tree. They can offer evidence that a couple was legally married, and may also indicate the bride's maiden name. Sometimes you'll even learn the bride and groom's date of birth or the names of the parents or other family members. Marriages also tend to generate a variety of documents, which increases your chances of finding a record that has survived through the years.

Marriage and Divorce Records

The most common civil record of marriage is the marriage license, issued to the bride and groom by the appropriate civil authority upon application for their marriage. Following the wedding ceremony, the license was returned by the minister or officiant, with the date and location of marriage to the county courthouse or town hall, to be recorded in the register. At the same time, an official certificate of marriage may have been issued to the couple; this certificate may be found among your family's papers. In some states, particularly the southern states, you may also encounter a precursor to the marriage license known as a marriage bond. This financial guarantee was made prior to the marriage by the prospective bridegroom (or a relative or friend of the groom or bride) to affirm that there was no moral or legal reason that the couple could not be married. In cases where the bride or groom were under the minimum legal age for marriage, you'll sometimes find a record known as the consent affidavit, a letter or form completed and signed by the parent or guardian giving permission for the underage individual to be married.

> **Critical Clicks**
> "Where to Write for Vital Records" (*www.cdc.gov/nchs/w2w.htm*) from the National Center for Health Statistics is a good starting place to learn about the availability of marriage and divorce records (as well as birth and death records) for the state you're researching. Vitalrec.com (*www .vitalrec.com*) also includes contact information and information on record availability for U.S. counties and parishes.

Civil marriage records in the United States are primarily found in the office of the county or town clerk. In some cases, however, older marriage records may have been transferred to the state archive, historical society, or library, while recent marriage records may only be available from the state vital records office. Individual state laws determine which agency is responsible. To further complicate matters, the date from which each state began to keep marriage records varies. Many states and territories were documenting marriages by 1880, but some did not officially record marriages statewide until well after 1900. In most cases, marriages were recorded at the town or county level prior to state registration, so you'll want to check county records as well. There is no nationwide index to marriage or other vital records in the United States.

Online, marriage records are becoming easier to find. The best place to start is FamilySearch.org, which offers free access to indexes and/or images of marriage records from many states and counties across the United States, as well as from elsewhere around the world. Fee-based site Ancestry.com also offers many marriage indexes and image collections. Alternatively, check the site for your state and county of interest at USGenWeb.org for links to marriage records, or do a search online for "marriage index" in your state and county or state and town (as applicable) of interest.

In the absence of a marriage license or certificate, evidence of a marriage may be found in other documents. If your ancestor was married in a church or other house of worship, the marriage was likely recorded in the parish register or church book, along with preliminaries such as the posting of marriage banns. Newspapers can also be a good source for marriage information, including engagements, announcements, photos, and even descriptions of the ceremony and reception. Look for a special section of the newspaper dedicated to wedding announcements, or in the local news or society pages. A marriage date may also have been recorded in the family Bible, on the back of a wedding photo, on a printed wedding or anniversary announcement, or in a letter, journal, or diary.

As with marriage records, divorce decrees relate to the family as a unit, and can often provide several details of genealogical value. These might include the wife's maiden name, the date and place of marriage, the dates of birth (or ages) of both parties to the divorce, the names and ages of any children, and the grounds for divorce. Divorce records are far less numerous than marriage records, however, and the manner in which divorces have been granted throughout history makes the records more difficult to locate as well.

Until the middle of the nineteenth century, divorce was rarely granted by the civil court. Instead, an act of the state legislature was necessary in most states, and it is among the records of these legislative acts where you'll find many early divorce proceedings. By the mid-1800s almost every state had enacted some type of divorce law, allowing for the "judicial" granting of a divorce. Most of these divorce decrees were issued in a court at the county level.

The particular court varies by location and time period, so divorce decrees may be found among the records of the Superior

Court, Circuit Court, Family Court, Chancery Court, District Court, or even the Office of the Prothonotary. Do a search online for divorce records in your state and county of interest to learn which court would have handled the process for the time period in which the divorce likely occurred. Most states also now require that a copy of the divorce certificate be filed with the state department that oversees vital records—a good alternative for divorces that have occurred since about the mid-twentieth century. References to a divorce may also be found in newspaper notices or among family papers.

Most marriage and divorce records online are available only in the form of indexes or abstracts, although increasingly websites are starting to add digital images as well. These indexes typically include the name of the bride, the name of the groom, and the date of the marriage or divorce. Unless the site also offers digital images of the actual marriage record, you should follow up by ordering or accessing the original record, as it will usually include additional details as well as offer additional verification of what you found online.

Birth and Baptismal Records

Because of privacy laws, birth records are generally the most difficult vital records to obtain and often cannot be found online for individuals born during or after the twentieth century. In fact, as with death records, official birth records were not even kept in many states until that time. For these more recent birth records it is usually best to start with your living family members. Because a birth certificate is often required as proof of identity, many people have a copy of their birth certificate among their papers.

Just because fewer birth records are available online than other vital records doesn't mean that you should discount finding them. FamilySearch.org has one of the largest collections of vital records online, including birth and baptismal records for dozens of U.S. states as well as many other countries around the world. Some of these free collections at FamilySearch are indexes only, while others also include digital images. Select "All Collections" from the home page of FamilySearch.org to bring up a full list of available historical records and then scroll down to your area of interest to see what's available.

Can I record the date of baptism in lieu of a birth date?
A baptism may have taken place days or years after the actual birth. For this reason it is important to record the date as a baptismal date, not a birth date. Most genealogy software programs include a special field for entering baptism or christening dates. In the birth field, just record the birth date as occurring before the date of baptism since that is all you truly know for sure, as in "bef. 13 April 1769."

Many state governments offer birth indexes and even certificate images online as well. Missouri, for example, offers a database of pre-1910 births (*www.sos.mo.gov/archives/resources/birthdeath*). Arizona offers not only an index but also images of the actual birth certificates (*http://genealogy.az.gov*) for births that occurred at least seventy-five years ago (so are no longer subject to privacy restrictions). West Virginia (*www.wvculture.org/vrr*) also has online images of birth records for selected counties and years. Ancestry.com offers a variety of online birth indexes among its subscription databases, including the North Carolina Birth Index (1800–2000), Kentucky Birth Collection (1852–1999), Minnesota Birth Index (1935–2002), and others. Check the website for the state archives, library, and/or historical society in your state of interest to see if they have put any birth records online. USGenWeb state and county sites will often include links to online birth indexes as well. Or try a search such as "birth records Arizona" to see what else might be available.

Older baptism and christening records are becoming increasingly easy to find online in countries such as England, Scotland, and France. In the United States, however, church records are much more scattered, and few baptisms and christenings have been transcribed and placed online. See Chapter 7 for more on researching in church records.

Unearth Wills and Estate Records

After you've learned the details of your ancestor's birth, marriage, and death, you'll want to check to see if he left behind any estate records when he died. While "estate" seems to imply a large amount of property, estates are actually the sum total of an individual's possessions, including both property and debts, left behind at the time of death. The amount of real or personal property required to necessitate a court proceeding is determined by state or local laws in effect at the time of death. Not everyone will have owned enough property to generate estate records, but your ancestor also didn't necessarily need to be well-off to have had his estate processed through the court system. If he had outstanding debts, property that needed to be divided, or anything else that needed to be settled after his death, it's likely that some record of that still exists.

Estate records document the processing and disbursement of an estate, whether the individual died testate (with a will) or intestate (without a will). If your ancestor left a will, an heir, creditor, or other interested party would normally present it to the court after his death. The court would hold proceedings and hear testimony to verify the validity of the will in a process known as probate. The court also officially appointed an executor—generally an individual or individuals named in the will by the testator—to handle the affairs of the estate. Often, executors were relatives or friends, but the executor or executrix could be anyone the testator considered trustworthy enough to handle his estate. Once the court approved the probate, the will was then generally recorded (transcribed) into a Will Book by the court clerk. In most cases, the original will (or a copy of it) also remained with the court, along with any other papers generated during the process of settling the estate, in a file often referred to as a probate packet.

When an individual dies without a will (which happens more frequently than you might think), the court generally appoints an administrator to handle the estate, and the distribution of property is made according to local law. These intestate proceedings, often called administrations, generate paperwork similar to the probate packets discussed previously, although they are sometimes referred to as administration packets.

What exactly can estate records tell you beyond the fact that your ancestor died? The documents found in an estate, administration, or probate packet might include a complete inventory of the property of the deceased, a list of debts and creditors, appraisals, receipts, newspaper notices calling for legal heirs to come forward, witness testimony, letters from attorneys representing heirs, a copy of the will (if one exists), and other miscellaneous papers related to the settlement of the estate. Each of these pieces of paper represents the potential for learning more about your ancestor—especially the names of relatives (including the married names of daughters) and where they were each living. The list of personal property can be especially interesting, filled with items such as crockery, feather beds, pigs, brooms, and the like, which provides insight into the life your ancestor lived.

Estate records can usually be found with the court records of the county where the deceased was last living. Early records may have been moved to other repositories, such as the state archives. Check with the county clerk or the local genealogical or historical society to learn where the estate records are maintained. Some wills, especially those prior to about 1850 or so, have been published online, either in image or transcription form. Try a search such as "Massachusetts wills online" and you'll turn up sites such as Wills of Our Essex County Ancestors (*www .essexcountyma.net/Wills*).

Other examples of online wills and estate records include Probate Database Search (*http://archives.delaware.gov/collections/probate .shtml*), an online searchable index to Delaware probate records from c. 1680 to c. 1925; the St. Louis Probate Court Digitization Project, 1802–1900 (*www.sos.mo.gov/archives/mojudicial/stl_history .asp*), a collaborative project of the Missouri State Archives and the St. Louis Probate Court; and the North Carolina State Archives (*www.archives.ncdcr.gov*), which includes digital images of wills dated between 1663 and 1790 in its MARS database as well as an index to estate records for some North Carolina counties.

Searchable databases on the no-frills SAMPUBCO website (*www.sampubco.com*) include indexes to more than 300,000 wills and probate files from more than a dozen U.S. states. Index searches are free, and you can order a digital or paper copy of most wills for a reasonable fee. Major genealogy sites such as FamilySearch.org and Ancestry.com also include will and estate records for various locations. Also check the local USGenWeb site and spend some time thoroughly searching in your favorite search engine to learn what may be available online for your area of research.

Genealogical Guidance

Laws in most Eastern and Midwestern states, derived from the common law of England, allowed the female widow a dower right, or share (usually one-third), of her husband's estate for her lifetime. When a mortgage or other debts existed, dower rights may have held up final settlement of the estate until after the widow's death. When no estate record is found, a search of land records may turn up the division of land necessary to give the widow her "dower third." Research dower rights in your state and time period of interest to learn more.

Chase Down Court Records

Most of the records previously discussed in this chapter, as well as land records and naturalization records can be found in the town hall or county courthouse where your ancestors lived. This is because the local courthouse is generally where official business was conducted—where your ancestor would have gone to apply for a marriage license, file settlement papers for an estate, record a land deed, pay his taxes, register to vote, or transact other business of day-to-day life.

In addition to the records mentioned in the preceding sections and discussed elsewhere in this book, court records also document cases involving civil and criminal actions. Don't be afraid to search these records because you're afraid of what you might find. It's not unusual to discover relatives sprinkled throughout court records for minor civil proceedings involving property line disputes, bastardy bonds, and unpaid debts.

Your ancestor did not even have to be accused of anything to appear in court records. He may have provided witness testimony for a friend or neighbor or posted bond money for a relative. Or he might be named in county business transactions—assigned as a local tax collector, or to oversee repair of a county road. Most of you will find few surprises, but even one or two unexpected mentions of your ancestor may help you in your search. If nothing else, court records can sometimes offer amusing fodder for your family history.

In the United States, every state has a system of local courts that handles most of the local business and transactions likely to have involved your ancestors. Use the Internet (e.g., Edgecombe County NC courthouse or South Dakota courts) to search for information on the court system and courts in the town or county where your ancestor lived. The USGenWeb site (*www .usgenweb.org*) is also a good starting point for learning about local courthouses and the location of their records. Consider also that your ancestor may have transacted at least some of his business in the courthouse that was most convenient to him, not necessarily the one that served the area in which he lived. Some business, such as the recording of land deeds, has to take place in the appropriate county or town, but other official business (e.g., obtaining a marriage license) can be handled at any county courthouse in some states. If you don't find court records in the most likely jurisdiction, expand your search to neighboring areas.

Critical Clicks

State and Local Government on the Net (*www.statelocalgov.net*) can be useful in locating official government websites, including those for the local court system. In addition, many states offer online directories of their county courts, such as the one found at Texas Courts Online (*www .courts.state.tx.us*). Most USGenWeb (*www.usgenweb.org*) county sites also provide contact information for the county courthouse.

The majority of court records will not be found online, but many court offices maintain some sort of virtual presence. The courthouse website may include information on the various offices within the courthouse and the records under their jurisdiction, the hours of operation, and, in some cases, details on how to request record lookups by mail or e-mail. Some courthouse offices, especially the Recorder of Deeds, may have indexes or other historical records online. The local library, historical society, or USGenWeb site may have published online guides or indexes to local court files. You can also check the Family History Library Catalog online to see if any court records have been microfilmed for your locality of interest, and request these for perusal through your local Family History Center.

Identify Adoptions and Orphans

Sometimes your own family history or the search for one of your ancestors is stalled because the circumstances of an ancestor's birth are shrouded in mystery. The first step in such a situation is the obvious one—to discover the names of the unknown birth parent or birth parents. If you believe the individual was formally adopted, the next step is to contact the agency or state that handled the adoption for a copy of the adoption order (in most states this information is sealed), or "non-identifying information," which, governed by state law and agency policy, may include important details that aren't considered revealing enough to identify the birth parents. This non-identifying information may include information on the adoptee (such as the date of birth and place of birth) and the birth parents (including a medical history, education level, religious affiliation, age at the birth, financial status, other siblings, and a physical description). Laws governing the release of identifying and non-identifying information about adoptions vary from state to state and country to country. Adoption.com offers a useful online guide to state adoption laws (*http://laws.adoption.com/statutes/state-adoption-laws.html*), including what information is available and where and how to access it.

The Internet is also especially helpful in adoption searches because of the access it provides to reunion registries that match up searching family members who have been separated by adoption, foster care, or other means. The International Soundex Reunion Registry (*www.isrr.net*) is the largest such mutual-consent registry. You can find links to others in the Registries section (*http://adoption.about.com/od/registries*) of the About.com Adoption site.

If you manage to locate the name of a birth parent, or at least enough family facts to offer the chance of being able to identify him or her, a variety of genealogy resources can be helpful in your search. Census records, newspaper notices and obituaries, online telephone directories, public record databases, the Social

Security Death Index, and other resources discussed throughout this book can be used.

Adoption is not the only thing that separates a child from his parents. It's not unusual to find a child sent to live with family members, or even neighbors, after a remarriage or the death of a parent. A child may also have been bound out as an apprentice to learn a trade. Children didn't even necessarily have to lose their parents to be considered orphans, placed for a time under the responsibility of the county or local government. There are many records of orphans, especially in large cities, with at least one living parent who for some reason wasn't able to support them. These children might be traced to a poorhouse or orphanage, or may have been reared by foster parents (related or unrelated) or even sent West on an orphan train.

A good place to search for information on orphans is the county courthouse. Many areas maintained an Orphans' Court that handled the sale and division of real estate arising from estates, as well as the guardianship of minor children. In areas without an Orphans' Court, these matters were usually handled by the Probate Court. A guardian was generally appointed by the court to take charge of a minor's property, not necessarily custody of the child; thus, a child could have a guardian even if one or both parents were alive. But many true orphans can be found in the records as well, as they needed to have a guardian appointed to manage their parents' estate for them until they became of age—generally age eighteen for females and age twenty-one for males. Orphans' Court proceedings may contain records of orphans being bound out as apprentices as well.

Sometimes you'll get lucky and an Internet search will turn up Guardianship and Orphans' Court records online. If not, check the FamilySearch Library Catalog online to see what guardianship and Orphans' Court records have been microfilmed for your area of interest, and search for the county courthouse online to learn how these records might be accessed directly.

Orphan asylums were established by governments, churches, and private charities, and so their records are understandably scattered. Check with the local library or historical society to see if they have information on orphanages that operated in the area, or do an Internet search such as "orphans western Pennsylvania." Cyndi's List (*www.cyndislist.com/orphans.htm*) is an excellent place to find links to online resources and records on orphans, orphanages, and orphan trains.

CHAPTER 7

Look Local

Pinpointing where your ancestors lived is crucial to locating the written records that detail their lives. It can show you which courthouse to check for civil records, where your ancestors worshipped, and even where they might be buried. Maps can help identify the ancestral homestead, visualize the places where your ancestors lived and died, and suggest possible migration routes once followed by your ancestors. Geography is also a powerful tool for distinguishing between two individuals with the same name.

Maps and Geography

Are you familiar with the area where your grandparents were born? You may know that it is a small Pennsylvania town called Shanksville, but you may not know what county it's in, or even whether it's located closer to Pittsburgh or Philadelphia. That's why the first thing you should do when you begin research in a new area is pull out a map. Online map services such as Yahoo! Maps (*http://maps.yahoo.com*), Google Maps (*http://maps.google .com*), or Bing Maps (*www.bing.com/maps*) all offer a host of features including address lookup, driving directions, and zoom and pan. Most also offer satellite imagery.

Locate a Lost Town, Village, or Creek

What if you can't locate your ancestor's town on a modern map? Place names change. Geographical and political boundaries shift.

Communities fall into disuse and disappear. Look for the answer in a gazetteer created during the time period of the document where you found the place name referenced. A gazetteer is a book that names and describes places in a given area during a given time period. With your mystery town's description and location from the gazetteer, you may be able to unearth a map from the period and identify the town's geographical location.

A variety of gazetteers can be searched and viewed online. One good modern gazetteer is Falling Rain's Global Gazetteer (*www .fallingrain.com/world*), a database of nearly 3 million populated places around the world, organized by country. Clicking on a location name takes you to a page with the latitude and longitude, several small maps, and a list of nearby cities and towns.

Historical gazetteers can be used to locate towns that do not exist in modern times. While most are tucked away in libraries and archival repositories, many historical gazetteers can also be accessed online. Sites such as Vision of Britain (*www .visionofbritain.org.uk*) include historical descriptions drawn from gazetteers. Try a search for "gazetteer" [your county, state, or region] to identify online gazetteers that may be useful in your research.

Critical Clicks

You must know who had jurisdiction over a location to find records, but political and geographic boundaries are constantly changing. To help ensure that you're looking in the right place, AniMap Plus for Windows, by Gold Bug Software (*www.goldbug.com/AniMap.html*), can display more than 2,300 color maps to show the changing county boundaries for each of the forty-eight contiguous states for every year since colonial times.

Explore the Lay of the Land—Virtually

Maps provide the opportunity to visually explore the places where your ancestors lived, as they existed at the time. A variety of maps can be of use to genealogists, including:

- Historical Maps—Historical maps come in many varieties. One of the most useful for genealogists is a historical land-owner's map, which shows property parcels along with the name of each landowner. Historical maps may also show churches, cemeteries, and other areas of interest. Thousands of historical maps are available online, some for free viewing and others for purchase. One of the largest free collections is the Perry-Castañeda Library Map Collection at the University of Texas at Austin (*www.lib.utexas.edu/maps*).
- Topographic Maps—Topo maps, short for topographic maps, are a favorite with many genealogists because of their high level of detail. These maps emphasize physical features on the surface of the earth, from mountains and streams to cemeteries and railroad lines. Large scale topo maps are sometimes so detailed you can see individual buildings, churches, and all navigable roads.
- Fire Insurance Maps—Fire insurance companies often requisition detailed maps of heavily populated areas to aid them in determining the risk factors in underwriting a particular property. These maps can be useful for genealogists because they depict building outlines, property boundaries, and street names for more than 12,000 American towns and cities. The Digital Sanborn Maps, 1867–1970, offers online access to a collection of more than 660,000 such maps. This database is available through subscribing libraries and institutions, so check with your local or state library to see if they offer it.

Land and Property Records

You've already learned in the previous section how to locate your ancestor's town on the map. Now, it's time to take a closer look at the property and community that he called home. Land is traditionally considered to be a valuable asset and, as such, great care has been taken in the recording of property ownership and transfer. People, understandably, want to have legal proof that their land belongs to them! For this reason, property records are among the most numerous records in existence, going back further in time and applying to more people than almost any other genealogical record.

Although they are overlooked by many beginners to family history research, land records are a favorite resource of most professionals for the valuable genealogical evidence they can provide. According to William Dollarhide in *"Retracing the Trails of Your Ancestors Using Deed Records"* (Genealogy Bulletin, Jan.–Feb. 1995), "nine out of ten adult white males in America owned land before 1850." He goes on to state that this claim still applies to more than 50 percent of white males today. With those odds, all genealogists with white American ancestors should be using land ownership records in their family history research. A land record can place an individual in a specific location and time that, in turn, can lead to further records or help distinguish between two individuals with the same name. Land records are also a good source for names and relationships of family members, such as when a group of heirs jointly sell a parcel of inherited land.

How can I identify my ancestor's property on a map?

With a protractor, ruler, and graph paper you can draw a plot of your ancestor's property based on the physical description in the deed or grant, a process known as land platting. Try it for yourself with the step-by-step instructions in *"Platting the Land of Your Ancestors"* (http://genealogy.about.com/cs/land/a/metes_bounds.htm), or use a computer program such as DeedMapper (www.directlinesoftware.com) by Direct Line Software to draw the plat map for you.

Land records include a variety of different document types, including patents, deeds, bounty land warrants, and homesteading grants. Depending on the type of record and the time period, these may be found at the national, state, county, or local level. To understand which records might tell you more about your family, you will need to become familiar with the types of land records created in your geographical area of interest during specific periods.

Who Owned the Land First?

The history of land acquisition and ownership in America could fill up an entire book. But it is also important to understand at least a little about how land was acquired, distributed, and transferred among governments and individuals in the area where your ancestor lived so you'll know what land records might be available and where they can be found. Search online for specific information on land history and ownership in your area, with a search query such as "history land Pennsylvania."

States where land was originally controlled and distributed by the colonial or state government are known collectively as the state-land states. These include the thirteen original colonies, plus Hawaii, Kentucky, Maine, Tennessee, Texas, Vermont, and West Virginia. As you might expect, these lands were surveyed and distributed in a variety of different ways. In some cases the government controlled the allocation of land, and in others this control was granted to a private citizen or citizens, such as the Lords Proprietors in North Carolina and the town proprietors of the New England states.

The majority of the state-land states, from Pennsylvania and New Jersey southward, continued the British survey system of metes and bounds to legally describe a piece of land. This system used local features such as trees, fences, stumps, and creeks to describe the property's boundaries. The distances along or between these features were usually described in poles, rods, or perches—all interchangeable with a distance of 16½ feet. In New England, this system was supplemented by the drawing up of town plats—most in a roughly rectangular shape. This town plat was granted by the government to a group of town proprietors who then oversaw the sale and distribution of lots within the town.

Land in the state-land states was generally first distributed by means of patents or grants. This patent/grant is the initial transfer of title from the government or proprietor to the patentee/grantee. It is the first title deed and the beginning of private ownership of the land.

Following the Revolutionary War, the new federal government got into the act—surveying and distributing the land under its control, also known as the public domain. The land in thirty states, often referred to as the federal-land states or public-land states, was initially controlled and surveyed by the U.S. government before its transfer into private hands. These public-land states were Alabama, Alaska, Arizona, Arkansas, California, Colorado, Florida, Idaho, Illinois, Indiana, Iowa, Kansas, Louisiana, Michigan, Minnesota, Mississippi, Missouri, Montana, Nebraska, Nevada, New Mexico, North Dakota, Ohio, Oklahoma, Oregon, South Dakota, Utah, Washington, Wisconsin, and Wyoming.

To keep things orderly, the government developed a new system for surveying its land prior to its being made available for purchase or homesteading, called the rectangular survey system or township-range system. The land was initially laid out into orderly squares organized along a meridian (imaginary line running from the North to the South Pole) and base line, which runs east and west. Meridian regions are divided into tracts of about 24 square miles, and these tracts are then divided into sixteen townships of about 16 square miles each. Each township is further subdivided into thirty-six one-mile square sections, each consisting of 640 acres, and these sections are further subdivided into smaller pieces such as halves and quarters called aliquot parts. Each piece of property in a public-land state is identified in this manner in relation to a particular base line and meridian line. More detailed explanation of the rectangular survey system can be found online by searching for "public land survey system."

In some states you'll run across several different systems of original land survey. For an extensive overview of land divisions and surveys in the United States, read *Land and Property Research in the United States* by E. Wade Hone.

Land in the public-land states was first distributed into private hands in a number of ways. The most common of these include homestead grants, military bounty warrants, and cash purchases of land.

Critical Clicks

Old land surveys are often hard to fit on a modern map because of magnetic declination, the difference between the true north (the axis around which the earth rotates) used for maps and magnetic north (the place the needle on a compass will point) used by land surveyors. Because the direction of magnetic north has changed over time, you'll need to adjust your survey plots to correct for this declination error. The National Geophysical Data Center (www.ngdc.noaa.gov/geomag) offers a handy historic declination calculator for just this purpose.

Locate Land Records Online

If your ancestor bought land from the federal government, you can do a free search for his land patent at the website of the General Land Office, U.S. Bureau of Land Management (*www.glorecords.blm.gov*). The database provides access to more than 2 million federal-land title records for the public-land states, issued between 1820 and 1908. These include images of both homestead and cash patents. You can also access images of serial patents (land title records issued between 1908 and the 1960s) and survey plats and field notes (dating back to 1810).

Patents are the final proof of land ownership, but there is also a wealth of information to be found in the paperwork generated by the land application process. This includes not only those who actually obtained patents, but the many who never completed the requirements or who had their application rejected. These application documents have been compiled into Land Entry Case Files, and are in the custody of the National Archives (*www.archives.gov/genealogy/land*). Some of these land files—especially the homestead applications—can contain significant genealogical information including the age or date of birth of the applicant, his marital status, name of the spouse, and size of the family. Land entry files can be ordered online from the National Archives (*www.archives.gov/research/land/*).

Since land in the state-land states was distributed by the colonial or state government, there isn't a nationwide database for these records. Instead, original land grant records can usually be found in the state archive or equivalent repository. They may also be found recorded in the county deed registers. Because of their historical value, many of these early land patents and grants are being digitized and placed online. Try a search such as historical "land records," or "land grants" plus the name of the state or county in question to learn what is available online for your area of interest.

Bounty land was granted by the federal government and eight states in return for military service. Many bounty land warrants can be searched and/ or viewed online.

Deeds transferring land titles between private citizens are maintained at the county or local level rather than the state level. Therefore, you won't find quite as many deed records online. Many counties do offer online access to recent deeds and other property information. Historical deeds, however, take time and money to digitize that many counties just can't afford. Exceptions, such as the New Hampshire County Registries of Deeds (*www .nhdeeds.com*) and Land Records in Maryland (*www.mdlandrec .net*), are becoming more and more common, however. Some early deeds may also be found in online collections hosted by state-level archives or historical societies. Do a search for county state deeds or check out the website of the Registrar of Deeds or Clerk of Court for the appropriate county and/or state to see what they may have online.

County land ownership atlases are another source for information on landowners in the United States. What sets these maps apart from other maps is that they include the names of individual landowners at a given point in time, as well as county and township boundaries and other important historical information. Check with the local Register of Deeds, library, or historical society to see if such landownership maps exist for the area and time period in which you're interested. Some can also be found online in major map collections, such as the Indexed County Land Ownership Maps, 1860–1918, (*http://search .ancestry.com/iexec/?htx=List&dbid=1127*) at Ancestry.com.

Historical Newspapers

Your family didn't necessarily have to be famous or wealthy to make the news—at least not after the introduction of the penny newspaper in 1833 made newspapers easily available to the masses. Important life events such as births, marriages, deaths, and funerals often appeared in the local newspaper, as did land transactions, court proceedings, school achievements, and other information on the everyday life of the area's inhabitants. Beyond the names and dates, newspapers frequently contain firsthand accounts of important events and issues, and reflect popular thinking and cultural attitudes of the time. Even the advertisements are enlightening, offering insight into local fashion, trends, and the cost of living.

Prior to the Internet, using historical newspapers to research family history was generally undertaken only by the most tenacious researchers. They just weren't easily available, often existing only on microfilm at the local or state library. Newspapers also don't typically come with an index, so newspaper research generally involves a lot of research and guesswork just to select the newspaper and issue(s) most likely to contain information of interest. Once the search has been narrowed to a particular newspaper and time period, newspaper research can still involve hours spent in front of a microfilm reader scrolling through page-by-page, skimming line after line.

Online access to historical newspapers has changed the scope of newspaper research, making it much more easily available to anyone interested in their family history. Many publishers and organizations have recently undertaken the digitization of historical newspapers in order to preserve and provide increased access to their rich history and commentary. The entire archive of the *New York Times*—dating back to its first issue in 1851—is just one such example of the many historical newspapers that have been made available for viewing via the Internet. These treasures of digital history present a great source for gaining knowledge about your family and the time and place in which they lived.

In addition to increased access, the digitization of historical newspapers allows for easier research with tools such as zoom, pan, and full-text search. The full-text search does come with a caveat, however. Most digitization projects use optical character recognition (OCR) technology to automatically recognize text within the digitized newspaper images. This process is much quicker and more cost-effective than manual indexing (can you imagine the effort the latter would take?), but does lend itself to inaccuracies. This is especially true for older newspapers where the typeface was a bit more flowery and may be harder for a computer to accurately decipher. Search results may include extraneous "matches" on words that the OCR technology believes are optically similar enough that they could be your target word. As a result, searching in historical newspaper databases can require quite a bit of creativity and patience, but the rewards are often immeasurable.

Genealogical Guidance
Don't limit yourself to births, marriages, and obituaries when researching your family in old newspapers. Some of the best finds may come from the society and neighborhood columns, where you can get little snippets about visiting relatives, children joining the military or leaving for college, people suffering or recovering from a serious illness, and trips to visit friends and family in other towns.

To locate historical newspapers online, first learn what paper(s) covered the location and time period in which you're interested. Then do a search for the paper by name and location plus terms such as "archive" or "historical." There are also websites that link to online papers and collections organized by state, such as Historic Newspapers Online (*http://genealogy.about .com/od/newspapers/tp/newspapers_online.htm*). Many historical newspapers are also found in the following large collections, which include content from newspapers across the United States as well as other countries such as Canada, Australia, and even Jamaica.

ProQuest Historical Newspapers

This collection of full-text and full-image articles from prestigious U.S. newspapers was first created in 2001 with the digitization of the *New York Times*. Other major newspapers now included in the fully searchable database include the *Chicago Tribune, Washington Post, Los Angeles Times, Atlanta Constitution, Boston Globe, Hartford Courant, New York Tribune, New York Amsterdam News, Pittsburgh Courier, Wall Street Journal*, and *Christian Science Monitor*. Every issue of each title includes the complete newspaper in downloadable PDF format and full-text search with a variety of advanced search options. This collection is only available through subscribing libraries and institutions, and is not available for individual subscriptions. Check with your local, college, or state library to see if they subscribe to any or all of the newspapers in this collection. Many offer free in-library and remote access to their patrons.

Newspaper Archive

This subscription-based service is one of the largest historical newspaper collections available online. The NewspaperARCHIVE database (*www.newspaperarchive.com*) contains more than 60 million full-page images from historical newspapers from around the world, ranging from the 1700s to the present. Coverage varies by newspaper, so use the Browse Available Papers feature to see which publications and dates are available before subscribing to a full-access membership. Online cancellation is available, but refunds are not offered for unused time. Selected papers from the NewspaperARCHIVE collection are available as part of a World Vital Records (*www.worldvitalrecords.com*) subscription.

Critical Clicks

Historical newspapers are available as part of the Ancestry.com subscription website. The Historical Newspaper Collection (*www.ancestry.com/search/rectype/periodicals/news*) offers access to more than 16 million pages from selected years of thousands of newspapers across the United States, United Kingdom, Canada, and Australia, dating back to the 1700s. Individual subscriptions to just the newspaper portion are not available; you have to subscribe to the entire Ancestry.com U.S. or World Record Collection.

GenealogyBank

A product of the information provider NewsBank, GenealogyBank (*www.genealogybank.com*) offers more than 480 million articles, obituaries, marriage notices, and birth announcements published in more than 4,300 historical U.S. newspapers, from 1690 through 1977. You can search the site for free and see brief excerpts that contain your search results, but you'll need to subscribe to view the entire article. A similar service, operating under the name America's GenealogyBank, is offered as a subscription service to libraries, so check to see if you have free access through your local or state library before subscribing.

Chronicling America: Historical American Newspapers

A joint project of the National Endowment for the Humanities (NEH) and the Library of Congress (LC), the National Digital Newspaper Program is a twenty-year plan to create a national digital resource of historically significant newspapers from all states and U.S. territories. The project's website, Chronicling America (*http://chroniclingamerica.loc.gov*), allows you to find information about American newspapers published between 1690 and the present, including the libraries that carry each title. The free database also allows you to search and read the currently digitized newspaper pages, which at this time includes newspapers published between 1860 to 1922 in nineteen states and the District of Columbia. As long as funding allows, the project will continue to expand its coverage.

Libraries and Societies

A stop at the public library of the community where your ancestor lived is a must for any family historian. Libraries are a gateway to rich primary source materials on the history and culture of the region they serve, as well as the people who lived in the area. The library is usually the local repository for archived newspapers, city directories, school yearbooks, and other resources specific to the community. Many larger libraries also maintain a local history section, with family histories, community and local history books, photographs, and records such as census enumerations, cemetery transcriptions, and marriage indexes.

Online, a library visit means an excursion to the library's website. Many libraries offer unique online content in the form of digitized original records, or transcribed indexes or databases. The University of Pittsburgh library (*http://digital.library.pitt .edu*), for example, provides access to historical maps and photos, transcribed census records, and the full text of more than 500 published works that relate to local Pittsburgh and Pennsylvania history. Another unique resource can be found on the website of the New York Public Library (*www.nypl.org*), where more than 600 Yiskor books (Holocaust memorial books) from the library's collection are available online in digitized format. Even smaller libraries may offer cemetery transcriptions or an index to obituaries that have appeared in their local paper. The Cleveland Public Library (*www.cpl.org*), which hosts an online Necrology File of cemetery records and newspaper death notices, is one such example. Collaborative databases, in which several libraries or societies pool their records and resources, are also becoming common online. A group of libraries in central and northeastern Ohio have banded together to create the regional MOLO Obituary Index (*www.ohiofamilysearch.org*).

Even libraries that don't have online records can be helpful in your research. Most library websites make at least a portion of their catalog available for searching online. Look for a link from the site's home page. You may also find information on submitting lookup or research requests. Many librarians are willing to do brief lookups in indexed books, databases, and clipping files, or provide a copy of an obituary if you can provide a name and date. In some cases this service may cost you a few dollars to cover expenses and postage, but it is well worth it. More and more librarians are also offering online "Ask a Librarian" assistance, either through e-mail or chat.

University and college libraries are sometimes overlooked by genealogists, but they often hold unique historical resources. They can have many unpublished genealogies and histories in their manuscript division, as well as the records of churches and businesses.

One tool used by many genealogists to locate library resources is WorldCat, a catalog of materials held in more than 10,000 libraries worldwide, including public, academic, and state libraries; archives; and historical societies. This includes special collections devoted to local history, which means you may find citations for historical newspapers, oral histories, family histories, cemetery records, historical photographs, family Bibles, town or county histories, and a wide variety of other materials. In 2006, WorldCat also opened a free Internet search portal to the public (*www.worldcat.org*). You can search it directly, and also access it through "find in a library" links for book results in sites such as Google Books and Amazon.

Churches and Schools

In just about every town, you can find a church and a school. Throughout much of history these buildings have served as the center of the community, a focus of daily life for area residents. For this reason, church and school records often provide intriguing insights into the lives and personalities of earlier generations. They may also supply concrete facts, such as dates of birth or baptism, marriage, and death, or proof of family relationships.

Religious Records

Church and synagogue records are a very valuable source for pre-1900 baptisms, marriages, and burials, but be prepared to face a few challenges. The existence of more than a hundred different religious denominations can make it difficult to determine the church with which your ancestor had an affiliation. Churches themselves have appeared, disappeared, and merged over time. Record keeping varies widely. Some records are in the custody of individual churches, others in diocesan collections, and still others in national archives or other repositories. Generally, there are few catalogs or indexes to these church records, and the vast majority cannot be accessed online. In most cases you'll find it necessary to visit the church or archives in person, or to hire a researcher.

To locate church records, you must first identify the denomination of your ancestor, and the actual church that she attended. Don't just assume that your ancestors practiced the same religion that you do today. It's very common to find individuals or families who have changed denominations. In rural areas, the choice of churches was generally limited, and residents may have attended the church or parish most convenient for them. Once you determine the religion, a directory may be able to help you pin down the church closest to where your ancestor lived.

When you have located the church, you next need to find out where the records are kept. Begin with an online phone directory or Internet search to see if the church still exists, and then contact it to learn about the availability of records for your time period of interest. If the church is no longer in existence, an e-mail or call to the local historical society or library, or to the regional headquarters for that denomination, may provide you with information. Many older church records have been published in book form or in local genealogical and historical periodicals. Look under your locality of interest in online library catalogs and in PERSI. The National Union Catalog of Manuscript Collections can be useful in locating church records held by libraries and historical societies.

One of the largest sources of transcribed and/or indexed church records online is the International Genealogical Index at FamilySearch (*www.familysearch.org*), which includes millions of extracted church records, primarily baptisms and marriages, from around the world. FamilySearch also offers digital images and transcriptions of many church and parish records from around the world in their Historical Records collection. Subscription genealogy sites such as Genealogy Today (*www.genealogytoday .com*) and Ancestry.com include databases such as church member lists, registers, and histories. An online search such as "church records Oakdale Pennsylvania" may turn up online databases, church histories, or other resources for church records in your locality of interest.

Even in the many cases where the actual church records are not online, you can do a lot of the background research on the Internet. The Family History Library has microfilmed records for many denominations that you can learn about by doing a place search in the online Family History Library Catalog. The websites for regional and national headquarters for many denominations offer information on the availability of records for family history research, as well as online directories of churches, parishes, or synagogues.

School Records

From the seventeenth century to the present day, schools and other educational institutions have created records that may have information about your ancestors, including registration records, class lists, alumni lists, transcripts, report cards, school censuses, and class photos. If your ancestor went to college you may be especially lucky, as colleges and universities tend to create, maintain, and preserve more comprehensive records than most primary and secondary schools. School fraternities and sororities also provide a potential source for records on such ancestors.

The one-room rural schoolhouse was a vital part of early American life, but these records, even if they have survived, may be hard to find. As the schools were closed, records may have been deposited with county or state repositories. Sometimes the local library or historical society may have these records, or know where they are kept. Twentieth-century school records are usually much more comprehensive, and can often be found by contacting the school or school district directly. Try your favorite search engine to find schools in a particular location, using a search such as "schools Lexington County South Carolina." The Board of Education in the state in which your ancestor attended school may also be of assistance in locating records. You'll often find, however, that many schools restrict access to personal information on people who may still be living. You may be able to get around these privacy issues by proving that you're a relative of the individual of interest, and that she is deceased.

As with church records, most school records cannot be accessed online. The previously mentioned subscription site Genealogy Today (*www.genealogytoday.com*) includes a number of transcribed school records and yearbooks. Ancestry.com includes a huge Yearbook Collection (*www.ancestry.com/yearbook*) of more than 10,000 school yearbooks spanning the years 1875 to 1988 among its subscription databases. Check the USGenWeb site for your county, as many have transcribed school records included among their online offerings. For university and college records, search their online library catalog to see what may be available in the school archives. Some collections of school records hidden away in libraries and archives may be found by searching the National Union Catalog of Manuscript Collections.

Yearbooks, school newspapers, and alumni registers and directories provide alternative avenues for research when the school records themselves are unavailable. If the school still exists—especially in the case of colleges, universities, or private schools—these resources may be available through the school library or alumni association.

CHAPTER 8

Seek Out Military Records

More than 42 million Americans, representing almost every generation, have participated in some type of wartime service. Men as young as sixteen and as old as sixty may have joined local militia units, making it likely that you'll discover at least one ancestor or relative with a military past. Military records can also document people who never actually served, such as the millions of young men who registered for the WWI and WWII drafts, but were never called up for duty.

Find Clues to Military Service

Begin your search for military records by talking with living relatives and reviewing the documents and other information you have already collected. The goal is to identify ancestors who may have participated in the military and, ultimately, to determine when and where the soldier served. Clues to an ancestor's military service may be found in the following:

- Family stories—If a relative says that your ancestor served in the military it is most likely true. Just keep in mind that memories get fuzzy with time, and the details may have been exaggerated or embellished a bit.
- Photographs—Search your family photograph collection for pictures of people in uniform. The type of photo and style of uniform can help determine the branch of the military and

the war or time period in which your ancestor served. Patches, pins, insignia, and even belt buckles may help determine rank or unit.

- Census records—Occupational references may indicate military service. The conspicuous absence of a male relative during wartime may also offer a clue. Surviving Revolutionary War pensioners or their widows were identified in the 1840 U.S. Federal Census and Civil War veterans or widows in the special 1890 Union Veterans Census (surviving only for the states of Kentucky [partial] through Wyoming, alphabetically, including D.C.). The 1910 federal census indicates whether the person was a "survivor of the Union or Confederate Army or Navy." The 1930 census indicates military service in major wars through World War I.

- Newspaper clippings—People were proud of their hometown heroes, and brief mentions of local soldiers often made the community papers.

- Journals and correspondence—Writing letters or keeping a diary offered a distraction from the boredom of military camp life and the terror of battle. Such letters or journals may be found among your family's belongings, or in a library or archive.

- Death records and obituaries—A soldier's obituary or death record may mention military service and provide details such as branch or regiment.

- Local histories—Published town or county histories often include stories and photos of local military units.

- Grave markers—A flag, emblem, engraving, or marker on your ancestor's gravestone may indicate military service. Many countries also honor their veterans with special markers.

Once you have determined that an ancestor served in the military, there are a wide variety of records that may help to document his service. These include military service records, draft registrations, medals and ribbons, pension papers, discharge papers, pay vouchers, casualty lists, unit rosters, and bounty land warrants. From these records you can learn such details as date and place of birth, age at enlistment, occupation, and names of immediate family members. The path you take in your search will depend upon when and where your ancestor served, whether he was regular army or with a volunteer unit, and whether he was an officer or enlisted personnel.

Compiled Military Service Records

For military ancestors who served prior to World War I, the compiled military service records are a good place to start. These are basically just what they sound like—an abstract of the available military information on an individual compiled from a variety of service-related records. Compiled military service records were originally begun in 1894 in an effort to reconstruct records of the American army and navy destroyed by fires in 1800 and 1814. The project eventually grew to cover all soldiers serving in volunteer units in wars between 1775 and 1902, including not only individuals from the American Revolution and War of 1812, but also those who served in various Indian conflicts, the Mexican War, the Civil War, the Spanish-American War, the Philippine Insurrection, and the Boxer Rebellion. A compiled military service record consists of a card with the soldier's name, rank, and unit, along with abstracted information taken from muster rolls, hospital records, pay vouchers, record books, orders, correspondence, and other records. This card is then placed in an envelope, or jacket. Sometimes original documents may also be included in the envelope. The compiled military service record will generally provide you with your ancestor's rank, unit, the state from which he served, the date enlisted, and the length of service. You may also find the age, residence, a physical description, and date of discharge or death.

The National Archives in Washington, D.C., is the official repository for federal military service records of personnel who served in the U.S. Army, Air Force, Navy, Marine Corps, or Coast Guard between the Revolutionary War and about 1912. This includes compiled military service records for Confederate Army soldiers. Military service records, including compiled service records, can be ordered online (*www.archives.gov/veterans/ military-service-records/pre-ww-1-records.html*), or by mail using NATF Form 86 (which you can download online). Indexes and/ or digitized images of these compiled service records can also be found online.

- Fold3 (*www.fold3.com*), in cooperation with the National Archives, offers subscription-based online access to the compiled military service records of soldiers who served in the American army during the Revolutionary War, as well as for Confederate Civil War soldiers (most of the Confederate records and some records of Union soldiers).
- Ancestry.com (*www.ancestry.com*) features an index to the compiled military service records for the volunteer soldiers who served during the War of 1812; index and images for compiled military service records for Revolutionary War soldiers; and indexes and some digitized images of Civil War service records, including those of the U.S. Colored Troops. Use the Ancestry Card Catalog to locate and search each specific database.
- The Civil War Soldiers and Sailors System (CWSS) (*www .itd.nps.gov/cwss*) offers a free index of more than 6 million Civil War Confederate and Union soldiers compiled from the General Index Cards of the compiled military service records

at the National Archives. Click on Soldiers or Sailors on the right-hand side to search for a name.

The War Department did not compile military service records for those who served in the regular army. The place to start researching pre–World War I enlisted Army personnel online is a set of helpful records titled U.S. Army Register of Enlistments, 1798–1914, at Ancestry.com (*http://search.ancestry .com/search/db.aspx?dbid=1198*), digitized from National Archives microfilm publication M233. U.S. Marine Corps Muster Rolls, 1798–1940 (*http://search.ancestry.com/iexec/?htx=List&dbid=1089*), is a collection of regular lists of Marine Corps personnel that also includes some early enlistment details. Additional information on pre–World War I records available for researching enlisted army personnel, as well as those who served in the navy and Marine Corps, can be found in the article "An Overview of Records at the National Archives Relating to Military Service." (*www.archivesgov/ publications/prologue/2002/fall/military-records-overview.html*).

What if I don't know whether I have an ancestor who was in the military?
If you have an ancestor of the right age at the right time to have served in a military conflict, it doesn't hurt to spend some time searching in military records—especially given the easy search capabilities of online databases. Just be careful not to assume that the individual you've found is your ancestor, especially if you discovered his name in an index, without following up in additional records.

Pensions and Bounty Land Warrants

The men and women who serve in the military are often compensated in some extra way for their service. In the case of the Revolutionary War, War of 1812, early Indian Wars, the Mexican War, and the Civil War, the records of these veterans' benefits—

pensions and bounty land warrant applications—are perhaps the most valuable resources available for genealogical researchers.

Military pensions were granted by the federal government or state government to disabled and needy veterans, to the widows or dependent orphans of veterans, or to veterans who served for a certain length of time and lived long enough to receive the pension benefits. Pension files are often rich in genealogical information, containing such facts as birth date and place, marriages, residence at time of application, property holdings, and names of minor children. Supporting documents, such as discharge papers, testimony from neighbors and fellow soldiers, marriage certificates, physician's reports, and family Bible pages, can sometimes be found included with pension files, especially in cases where the veteran had difficulty proving his pension eligibility. These are the thick, juicy files that all genealogists drool over!

The federal government, and some states, granted free land known as bounty land to veterans as an inducement or reward for service in the military. Bounty land warrants were issued from the colonial period until 1858, when the program was discontinued, to veterans of the Revolutionary War, War of 1812, and Mexican War. Bounty land was not available for Civil War soldiers. Veterans or their heirs could claim this free land by filing an application, known as a bounty land warrant application. If the application was approved, the individual was given a warrant that he could later exchange for land on which he could settle. The government set aside certain land districts in the frontier areas where veterans could redeem their warrant for bounty land. Many historians believe that this was designed to lure the battle-trained soldiers and their families into areas where they could serve as a buffer against Indian attacks. Most veterans were too smart to fall for that ploy, and instead chose to sell their land warrants to speculators. Therefore, your veteran ancestor may have applied for a bounty land warrant, but never received title to or settled on bounty land.

Many of the early Revolutionary War bounty land application files from 1789 to 1800 were destroyed in a War Department fire. Most of the surviving applications relating to Revolutionary War and War of 1812 service have been combined with the pension files because they contain similar types of information.

An excellent online resource for these records is the Revolutionary War Pensions database at Fold3.com, with both a name index and digitized images reproduced from National Archives microfilm publication M804. If Fold3.com isn't available to you, then check to see if your local library subscribes to HeritageQuest Online. There, the Revolutionary War Pension and Bounty-Land Warrant Application Files database, which also includes an index as well as digitized copies of the original handwritten records, was taken from NARA microfilm M805, which reproduces selected portions of the pension and bounty land applications filed by Revolutionary War veterans or their heirs between 1800 and 1906, generally about ten pages or fewer per file of the most genealogically significant documents. If you find an ancestor in the HeritageQuest database, you really want to consider accessing the complete file at Fold3.com as well.

FamilySearch.org (Civil War Pension Index Cards—free) and Fold3.com (Civil War and Later Veterans Pension Index—subscription) each host a searchable name index and images of the pension index cards of Union Civil War veterans reproduced from NARA microfilm T-289, Organization Index to Pension Files of Veterans Who Served Between 1861–1917, with more than 3 million index entries documenting the pension applications of soldiers, sailors, and their widows. A similar Civil War Pension Index is available on Ancestry.com (*http://search.ancestry.com/ search/db.aspx?dbid=4654*), reproduced from NARA microfilm T-288, General Index to Pension Files, 1861–1934. It's worth checking both the T-288 and T-289-based indexes, as they each may contain slightly different information.

The War of 1812 Pension Project (*www.fgs.org/1812*), a collaboration of the Federation of Genealogical Societies and the National Archives, is undertaking to digitize and put online the 180,000 pension files of soldiers who served in the War of 1812. A search engine query such as genealogy pension will turn up additional online sources of military pension records, such as the USGenWeb Archives Pension Project (*www.usgwarchives.org/pensions*).

Copies of military pension claim files for military service from the American Revolution up to just before World War I (1775 to 1912), and bounty land warrant applications for federal military service prior to 1856, can be ordered online from the National Archives (*www.archives.gov/veterans/military-service-records/pre-ww-1-records.html*), or by mail using NATF Form 85. They will only copy up to 100 pages, however, and it's not at all uncommon for Civil War pension files in particular to run in excess of that, so you may get better results by hiring a professional genealogist to obtain the file in person from the National Archives. It's important to note that the National Archives pensions and bounty land warrants are based on federal (not state or Confederate) service. Pension records for Confederate soldiers are discussed in the Civil War section later in this chapter.

Discover Revolutionary and Civil War Ancestors

There's something a bit special and awe-inspiring about having an ancestor who served in the American Revolution or Civil War—knowing that someone from whom you descend participated in the struggle to win the freedoms you enjoy today. Whether you agree with their reasons for fighting or the side for which they fought, it can be a real source of pride to have ancestors who were willing to fight and die for a cause they so strongly believed in. Learning about these ancestors and their beliefs can also help connect you to a very important part of this nation's history in a way that almost nothing else can.

The American Revolution

Whether you're interested in joining a lineage society such as the Daughters of the American Revolution or Sons of the American Revolution, or just want to learn more about possible Revolutionary ancestors, a good place to start your online search is the Genealogical Research System of the Daughters of the American Revolution (*www.dar.org*). Select Library from the top tab and then Online Research in the left-hand navigation to access the database of Revolutionary Patriots, men and women who have been accepted by the DAR genealogical staff as having contributed to the cause of American independence between 1774 and 1783, as well as other useful resources. If you find your ancestor listed as a Revolutionary Patriot, you can also use their website to order a copy of the most recent DAR application or file for your patriot ancestor.

Critical Clicks
The U.S. Department of Veterans Affairs (VA) will furnish, upon request and at no charge to the applicant, a government headstone or marker for the grave of any eligible deceased veteran in any city around the world, including those buried in private cemeteries. Learn more about the eligibility requirements and how to apply for a military marker from the Department of Veterans Affairs (*www.cem.va.gov/cem/hm_hm.asp*).

Next, check out Fold3 (*www.fold3.com*), which provides subscription-based access to a variety of digitized Revolutionary-era records from the National Archives. These include the previously mentioned compiled service records and pension records, as well as Revolutionary War muster rolls and payrolls and the papers of the Continental Congress.

A few other excellent online databases for Revolutionary-era research include:

- American Genealogical-Biographical Index (*www.ancestry.com*)—Includes indexes to numerous Revolutionary War–related publications. A subscription is required.
- A Century of Lawmaking for a New Nation (*http://memory.loc.gov/ammem/amlaw*)—This special collection in the free online American Memory exhibit of the Library of Congress includes some very interesting Revolutionary War pension petitions and other sources for information on Revolutionary-era individuals. Follow the links to American State Papers and the U.S. Serial Set.

Many Revolutionary War soldiers fought in the state militia, and their records will usually be found among the appropriate state's records, not in the National Archives. Various state archives, historical societies, and other organizations have posted some of their state Revolutionary War records online. Examples include Pennsylvania Revolutionary War Military Abstract Card File Indexes (*www.digitalarchives.state.pa.us*) and the Kentucky Secretary of State Revolutionary War Warrants index (*http://apps.sos.ky.gov/land/military/revwar*). Do a search in your favorite search engine for "revolutionary war" +your state to find available records and documents.

A discussion of American Revolution research wouldn't be complete without a reminder that there was another side to the war. You may have ancestors who were Loyalists, or Tories—colonists who remained loyal subjects of the British crown and actively worked to promote the interest of Great Britain during the American Revolution. After the war ended, many of these Loyalists were driven from their homes by local officials or neighbors, and almost all moved on to resettle in Canada, England, Jamaica, and other British-held regions. The Online Institute for Advanced Loyalist Studies (*www.royalprovincial.com*) provides an excellent starting point for further research into Loyalist ancestors.

The Civil War

The Civil War marked the most tragic chapter of American history. As with the Revolutionary War, the conflict tore apart families, friendships, and even towns. These divided loyalties mean that you may find you have ancestors who fought on both sides.

If your ancestor was born between about 1805 and 1847, chances are good that he may have fought in the Civil War. Even men in their sixties and boys in their early teens participated. But where did he serve, and for which side? The three most valuable pieces of information necessary for researching a Civil War ancestor are the soldier's name, whether he served for the Confederate or Union Army, and the state from which the soldier served. With this information you can determine what types of records are available that might tell you about your ancestor and where he is located. Remember, there were two national governments in effect during those years—the federal government of the United States and the Confederate States of America. Combined with the massive destruction of property, especially in the South, this means that many of the existing records have been left fragmented and scattered among the National Archives, state archives, lineage societies, and other repositories. Plenty of excellent Civil War records do exist; they are just not all in one place. Therefore, the biggest hurdle in Civil War research is often in knowing where to look.

The first step in documenting your ancestor's Civil War service is to search service records and rosters for his name. The previously mentioned Civil War Soldiers and Sailors System (*www.itd .nps.gov/cwss*) is the best place to start. Here you can learn your ancestor's regiment, allegiance, and rank. With these facts you can dig further into the database and bring up information on his unit. The subscription-based American Civil War Research Database (*www.civilwardata.com*) is another excellent resource for researching Civil War soldiers.

If you find your ancestor in either the Civil War Soldiers and Sailors database or the American Civil War Research Database, you can often learn more by accessing his complete compiled military service record. These can be ordered online through the National Archives. Alternatively, Fold3 has digitized these files and placed them online where you can access them a bit cheaper and a lot quicker!

Why aren't Confederate ancestors found in the National Archives?

Actually, the National Archives does hold the compiled military service records of Confederate officers and enlisted men, containing information taken from documents captured by Union forces and from Union prison and parole records. Because the Confederate States of America operated as a separate government, however, Confederate pensions and bounty land were authorized by the individual Confederate or border states and the records are generally found in the respective state archives.

Once you've confirmed your ancestor's Civil War service you can often learn further details about him in pension records. If he lived long enough, the chances are good that your Union Civil War ancestor applied for a pension. If not, his widow or dependents likely applied. These federal pension records are available from the National Archives and can be ordered online. As previously mentioned, both Ancestry.com and Fold3.com offer subscription-based access to general indexes of these Union pension files. Fold3 also has a small subset of the complete Civil War Widows' Pension files online.

The federal government did not offer pensions to Confederate soldiers until 1959, by which time the majority of Confederate veterans and their widows were deceased. Most Confederate states administered their own pension program, however. The veteran was eligible to apply for a pension in the state in which he lived, regardless of the unit in which he served. Generally, only indigent or disabled Confederate veterans, or their dependents, were eligible for pensions. The majority of these pension records can be found in the appropriate state archives, library, or historical society.

As with other genealogy records, a good search engine query such as [your state] "civil war" genealogy or [your state] "civil war" records will turn up a variety of useful databases and resources such as the Roster of Wisconsin Volunteers, War of the Rebellion, 1861–1865 (*www.wisconsinhistory.org/roster*), and the Texas State Library and Archives Commission Index to Confederate Civil War Pension Applications (*www.tsl.state.tx.us/ arc/pensions/ index.php*).

Research Twentieth-Century Conflicts

If you're new to tracing your family tree, you may not yet have gone back far enough to explore the rich records generated by the Civil War and American Revolution. That doesn't mean you can't benefit from military records, however. World Wars I and II, the Korean War, and the Vietnam War all generated records that are useful for genealogical research.

Was He Drafted?

Almost every male U.S. resident between the ages of eighteen and forty-five completed a World War I Draft Registration Card in one of three separate draft registrations conducted in 1917 and 1918. These records include vital information on more than 24 million men—whether native-born, naturalized, or alien—born between about 1873 and 1900. More than 80 percent of the men who registered for the draft never actually ended up serving in the military, so they can be a valuable resource for learning about your nonmilitary ancestors as well.

Each of the registrations used a different form with a slight variation in the questions asked. All three include the individual's full name, home address, date of birth, age in years, and occupation; the name and address of his employer; his citizenship status; a physical description; the city/county and state of the local draft board; the date of registration; and the signature of the applicant. The three registrations also include the following additional information:

1. June 5, 1917 (all men between the ages of twenty-one and thirty-one): Additional information included exact place of birth (usually including town), number of dependents, marital status, previous military service, and grounds for exemption.

2. June 5, 1918 (men who reached the age of twenty-one between June 5, 1917, and August 24, 1918): Additional information included exact place of birth, nearest relative's name and address, and father's birthplace.

3. September 12, 1918 (all men aged eighteen to forty-five who hadn't previously registered): No birthplace this time, but did ask for the name and address of the nearest relative. The original WWI draft registration records are housed at the National Archives–Southeast Region near Atlanta, Georgia. The records have also been microfilmed and can be accessed through the Family History Library. Fully indexed, digitized copies of the original World War

I draft registration cards can be accessed online as part of the subscription-based offerings at Ancestry.com. Alternatively, you can request scanned reproductions of the World War I draft registration cards online through the National Archives Order Online service.

World War II draft records also exist, but registration cards from the fourth registration are the only ones currently available to the public due to privacy restrictions. This fourth registration, often referred to as the "old man's registration," was conducted on April 27, 1942, and registered men who were born on or between April 28, 1877, and February 16, 1897 (ages forty-five to sixty-four), and not already in the military. The original draft cards are held by each state's National Archives regional branch, and are also available on microfilm from NARA and/or the Family History Library. Ancestry.com offers an online, searchable database with digitized images of the currently available WWII draft registration cards. FamilySearch.org also hosts the fourth registration of World War II draft card images for free. Unfortunately, the records for many of the southeastern states were destroyed before they were copied and will never be available. These include Alabama, Florida, Georgia, Kentucky, Mississippi, North Carolina, South Carolina, and Tennessee.

As useful as they are for locating information about ancestors who may have served in the military, World War I and World War II draft registration cards do not include any details of actual military service. For those men who did enlist in the military following their registration in either draft, you should turn to military service records for further information.

Request Your Ancestor's Military Service Record

Service records consist of the information that the government collects and keeps on any military personnel. This might include the soldier's enlistment/appointment, duty stations and assignments, training, performance, awards and medals, disciplinary actions, separation, discharge, and retirement. Military service records are available for enlisted men who served in the regular army throughout America's history, as well as discharged and deceased veterans of all services during the twentieth century.

Military records from just before World War I to the present are held in the National Military Personnel Records Center (NPRC) in St. Louis, Missouri. Access to many of these records is limited by privacy laws and, as such, they are not available online. Military veterans and the next of kin of deceased military veterans can order copies of these records through EVetRecs (*www.archives.gov/veterans/evetrecs/index.html*), an online military personnel records request system.

Unfortunately, a disastrous fire at the NPRC on July 12, 1973, destroyed an estimated 16 to 18 million of these military personnel files. This includes approximately 80 percent of the U.S. Army personnel records for persons discharged between November 1, 1912, and January 1, 1960, and 75 percent of U.S. Air Force personnel records for persons discharged between September 25, 1947, and January 1, 1964, alphabetically through Hubbard, James E. These records were never duplicated or microfilmed prior to the fire, so there are no surviving copies. The NPRC will attempt to reconstruct a destroyed service record upon the request of a veteran or surviving family member.

Search Conflict-Specific Databases

A number of databases are available online for researching veterans of World War I, World War II, Korea, Vietnam, and other twentieth-century conflicts. One of the largest is the World War II Army Enlistment Records File in NARA's Access to Archival Databases (*http://aad.archives.gov/aad*). This freely searchable database contains information on about 8.3 million men and women who enlisted in the U.S. Army during World War II. These records contain a great deal of useful information about the enlistee, including year and place of birth, civilian occupation, marital status, education, and enlistment details. For those who died during World War I, World War II, or the Korean War, the American Battle Monuments Commission (*www.abmc.gov*) maintains a variety of databases of Americans interred overseas, missing in action, or lost at sea.

CHAPTER 9

Trace Your Immigrant Ancestors

Virtually all Americans are descended from immigrants. Some arrived via the Bering Strait during prehistoric times. Europeans, mostly English, came during the seventeenth and eighteenth centuries to colonize and settle the rich, new land. Still others fled famine and political unrest in Northern and Western Europe. More than 500,000 were brought unwillingly as slaves between 1619 and 1808. Millions more arrived by foot, car, bus, train, ship, and plane from all over the globe. All told, more than 50 million immigrants have been welcomed to the United States, so at some point your family tree will branch out beyond America's shores.

Find the Birthplace of Your Immigrant Ancestor

One of the biggest challenges in tracing your family history is locating information about immigrant ancestors. Because most foreign records are kept at the town level, discovering the name of your immigrant's town, county, or parish of origin is an important goal. Without this information, it will be very difficult to expand your research to your ancestor's native country.

Begin by learning as much as you can about that person. Talk to living family members and search through family possessions or histories for evidence of the family's origins. Are there any marriage records, death certificates, naturalization certificates, photographs, funeral cards, newspaper clippings, military records, or letters from relatives back in the old country? Was the family surname changed at some point in the past? What religion did the family practice and/or what church did they attend? Are there any other clues that family members can think of that may point to the family's origins?

If that doesn't provide the information you're looking for, turn your search to public records, including vital, tax, census, land, military, and probate records. Begin with your immigrant ancestor's death. Death certificates, probate records, obituaries, and tombstones may indicate a birthplace or, at least, a country of origin. If your ancestor died after about 1962, try a search in the Social Security Death Index, as mentioned earlier in this book. With the information from the index you can order a copy of the application he filled out when he applied for a social security card. These forms almost always give place of birth and names of parents.

After that, a good place to search for information on immigrant ancestors is in the federal census schedules. Begin with the most recent census in which your ancestor appeared and work your way back to 1850, or as far as you can. The 1900, 1910, 1920, and 1930 censuses each indicate the person's year of immigration to the United States and naturalization status ("Al" for alien, "Pa" for "first papers," and "Na" for naturalized). These may help lead to passenger manifests or naturalization records for your immigrant ancestor. The 1850 to 1930 censuses indicate the person's state or country of birth, which can help narrow down your search. The 1880 to 1930 censuses also indicate the parents' birthplaces. Sometimes you get lucky and find a census taker who writes in the town or county as well!

With the information you glean from census records you can often begin a search for your immigrant ancestor in passenger lists and naturalization records (discussed in detail later in this chapter). Early naturalization and passenger records generally only provide the country of birth, but more recent naturalization records and passenger records (after about 1906) will usually indicate the town of birth as well.

Genealogical Guidance
Expect inconsistencies in place of origin. Constantly shifting political and geographical boundaries in Eastern Europe, for example, may have led to various countries being recorded as the birthplace of your ancestor. It's also not uncommon for immigrants from small villages to say they hailed from a better-known town or city in the vicinity. Investigate multiple sources that list birthplace for verification, if possible, including records for collateral relatives who also immigrated to America.

Plunge Into Passenger Lists

Few achievements in family history research are as fulfilling as discovering your ancestor's name on a passenger list—often the first tangible evidence of her existence in America. If you've done your research on your immigrant ancestor, locating the actual manifest may tell you nothing new. But just seeing her name listed alongside those of her fellow passengers, and identifying the name of the ship she came over on, is a satisfying experience. And sometimes, especially with twentieth-century immigrants, the passenger list may provide that one clue you need to untangle your immigrant ancestor's story.

Most immigrants to the United States enter through a port city or border-crossing checkpoint. If they entered legally and under normal circumstances, some type of paperwork was generally completed to document their entry. The content and thoroughness of this information varies by time period, and the immigration records that were generated can be classified into several broad categories.

Passenger Arrivals Prior to 1820

From early colonial times through 1819, documentation of passenger arrivals was under the jurisdiction of the colonies (and later, states). The primary concern of these entities was the taxation of goods—not the transport of passengers—and ships' captains were not always required to maintain passenger lists. Documentation of passengers from this time period may come from a variety of sources, including: (1) a listing on the ship's cargo manifest, (2) notation of passengers in the ship's log, (3) publication of passenger arrivals in the local newspaper, and (4) lists created upon departure from the country of origin. In addition, names of ship passengers may be noted in private journals, in the archives of immigrant-sponsoring societies or organizations, or even attached to medical reports for ships quarantined due to onboard disease.

Could my ancestor's name have been changed at Ellis Island?
Many immigrants arriving in America did ultimately change their names, to avoid prejudice or to better assimilate into society. This name change most likely did not occur upon their arrival in the United States, however. It wasn't the job of Ellis Island and other port officials to write down names. Instead, they checked the immigrant's paperwork against the passenger list created by the shipping company at the port of departure, not the port of arrival.

Pennsylvania offers one notable exception to the lack of required passenger documentation prior to 1820. Beginning in 1727, Pennsylvania required that all non-British immigrants be identified and take an oath of allegiance. Generally only adult male passengers over the age of sixteen were recorded, although some of the later lists also include women and children. These early Pennsylvania lists, totaling about 65,000 passengers of primarily German and Swiss descent, were originally compiled in 1962 by Ralph B. Strassburger and William J. Hinke. The three-volume series of books titled Pennsylvania German Pioneers has since been reprinted. Some of the passenger lists from this series have been transcribed and made available online at Pennsylvania German Pioneers Passenger Lists (*http://freepages.genealogy.rootsweb.com/~pagermanpioneers*). Ancestry.com offers a searchable database of the entire series as part of its U.S. subscription package.

There is no central repository for pre-1820 passenger records, and many of them have been lost or destroyed. Those that remain are scattered in libraries, historical societies, archives, museums, and private hands. The majority of the known pre-1820 records have been published in books and journals. Two excellent bibliographic reference works detail many of these pre-1820 passenger records: Harold Lancour's *A Bibliography of Ship Passenger Lists, 1583–1825*, third edition, and William P. Filby's *Passenger and Immigration Lists Bibliography, 1538–1825*, second edition.

William Filby has also indexed many of these published pre-1820 passenger lists in his *Passenger and Immigration Lists Index*. This work, originally published in three volumes and supplemented annually, names about 2.25 million pre-1820 immigrants. It can be consulted in many major libraries and is also available online as part of the Immigration Collection at the subscription site Ancestry. com. Additional sources for online research of pre-1820 passenger lists can be found in genealogist Joe Beine's bibliography of books, CD-ROMs, and online databases for lists of U.S. passenger arrivals before 1820 (*www.germanroots.com/1820.html*).

Another online resource for early passenger lists is GenealogyBank.com. This subscription-based site also offers a free list of passengers who arrived in the United States from October 1, 1819, to September 30, 1820 (*www.genealogybank.com/ free*), covering arrivals at thirty-four ports in fourteen states and the District of Columbia.

Customs Passenger Lists, 1820–1891

The federal government did not begin keeping a record of passenger arrivals until 1820, after Congress passed the Steerage Act of 1819. This act regulated the transport of passengers from foreign ports to the United States, and required ships' captains to submit a list of their ship's passengers to the customs collector at the port of entry. From January 1, 1820, to approximately 1891, these passenger lists were kept by the U.S. Customs Service and are thus often referred to as customs lists or customs passenger manifests. They generally provide a minimum amount of information on the immigrant, including:

- Name of the ship and its master
- Port of embarkation
- Date and port of arrival
- Passenger's name
- Passenger's age
- Passenger's gender
- Passenger's occupation
- Passenger's nationality

The U.S. Immigration Service Assumes Control in 1891

The number of immigrants entering the United States grew so quickly that Congress passed the first federal law regulating immigration in 1882. Nine years later, the Immigration Act of 1891 moved jurisdiction of the immigration process to the federal government, under the new Superintendent of Immigration (which became the Bureau of Immigration and Naturalization in 1906). This office was responsible for processing all immigrants seeking admission to the United States, for deciding to admit or reject immigrants, and for implementing national immigration policy.

As part of this implementation, "immigrant inspectors" were stationed at major American ports of entry for the purpose of collecting and reviewing the arrival manifests, referred to as immigration manifests or immigration passenger lists. These lists began about 1891 and continued until 1957, the exception being the port of Philadelphia, whose immigration passenger lists began in 1882. Although "Customs Passenger Lists" became

"Immigration Passenger Lists," the information included on the two lists is virtually identical until 1893. Beginning that year, the federal government issued new standard forms with sixteen additional columns of information. Later revisions added even more information. These post-1892 passenger lists include the same information found on the earlier lists, along with the following additional details:

- Marital status
- Last town of residence
- Final destination in the United States, often including name of relative or friend
- Whether the passenger could read and write
- Amount of money the passenger was carrying
- Passenger's state of health
- Race (from 1903)
- Place of birth (from 1906)
- Personal description (from 1906)
- Name and address of nearest friend or relative in the old country (from 1907)

As with almost any rule, there are a few exceptions. One French immigrant's arrival in the United States is recorded on a 1946 passenger list, but the list itself provides none of the information you might expect for an immigrant at that time—listing only her name, age, and an application number. This is because she is listed along with more than 800 other women and their children on that ship as "applying for admission to the United States under the Act of December 28, 1945." The War Brides Act, which helped facilitate admission into the United States for foreign-born spouses of U.S. soldiers who married overseas during World War II, is just one of many such exceptions that may impact the information you'll find recorded on a passenger list.

Keep in mind as you research that passenger records are not always available for all ports during all time periods. The port of Galveston, Texas, for example, lost the majority of its immigration records from the years 1871 to 1894 in the great Galveston Hurricane of 1900. The National Archives holds a few extant passenger lists for San Francisco, but the official lists for that port were destroyed by fire in 1851 and 1940. Don't let this keep you from searching, however! Sometimes you'll find your ancestor immigrating through a port other than the one you expect, or you may find an alternate resource (such as an outbound passenger list from the departure city) that lists your ancestor. Online immigration indexes make searching much easier than it used to be, often allowing you to search across records of multiple ports in one step.

Locate Passenger Records Online

The National Archives is the primary repository for immigration records for passengers arriving from foreign ports between approximately 1820 and 1982. Microfilm copies of passenger lists up to about 1960 are available at the National Archives building in Washington, D.C. Some are also available at NARA's regional branch facilities, and most of the microfilms can be borrowed through your local Family History Center. Just a few years ago, this was the only feasible method for doing research in passenger lists. Now, however, the majority of U.S. passenger records prior to about 1960 are also available for online research through a variety of sources.

One of the first large collections of passenger records to go online was the Ellis Island database (*www.ellisislandrecords.org*), which includes transcripts and digital images for arrivals at Ellis Island and the port of New York between 1892 and 1924. The immigration passenger lists prior to 1897 for the port of New York were actually destroyed in an 1897 fire at Ellis Island, but the customs passenger lists that were also kept for those years do survive and are included in the Ellis Island database. This free, searchable database includes approximately 22 million total records, along with ship photos and stories of the immigrant experience.

Genealogical Guidance

Be sure when looking at online ship passenger manifests to click through to the next page in case the passenger information extends over more than one page (which it does for most post-1892 manifests). Click through to the end of the manifest as well—you may find a list of individuals who died during the voyage, or who were detained for health or other reasons, such as "likely to become a public charge" (fairly common for young children or women traveling solo with no visible means of support).

The "other" major New York port, Castle Garden, served as America's first official immigrant receiving station from 1855 through 1890, before being succeeded by Ellis Island in 1892. The Castle Garden website (*www.castlegarden.org*) offers a free searchable database of 10 million of the passengers who arrived at Castle Garden. These are transcriptions only, but Ancestry .com subscribers can access digital copies of the Castle Garden manifests.

The subscription-based U.S. Immigration Collection at Ancestry.com (*www.ancestry.com*) is the largest online source for passenger lists, including digital copies of virtually all readily available U.S. passenger lists from 1820 to 1960, as well as an index to the more than 75 million passenger names and 26 million crew names found on these lists. Nearly 80 percent of these records come from the receiving stations at the port of New York—primarily Ellis Island (including arrivals during years not included in the free Ellis Island database discussed earlier in this section). The major ports of Boston, San Francisco, New Orleans, Philadelphia, and Baltimore are also represented in this collection, along with more than 100 other U.S. ports of arrival.

The records are available only to subscribers, or through a free trial offer.

Some of the other immigration databases and passenger lists that can be found online include:

- Immigrant Ship Transcribers Guild (*www.immigrantships .net*)—This site offers free access to more than 8,000 individual passenger manifests transcribed by volunteers. Click on the Passenger Lists and Special lists links to view and search the available records.
- National Archives (*http://aad.archives.gov/aad*)—The Access to Archival Databases (AAD) includes in its Passenger Lists a searchable database titled "Passengers Who Arrived at the Port of New York During the Irish Famine," documenting primarily Irish immigrant arrivals during the period January 12, 1846, to December 31, 1851. About 70 percent of the passenger records list Ireland as the native country.
- Galveston Immigration Database (*www.galvestonhistory.org/ Galveston_Immigration_Database.asp*)—More than 130,000 passengers who disembarked at the port of Galveston between 1846 and 1948 are included in this free, searchable database. Not included are arrivals between the years 1871 and 1894, along with a few during 1900 because of the destruction of records in the 1900 hurricane.

Emigration (Outbound) Lists

Your ancestor most likely also left records behind in the old country when he came to the United States. These emigrant records created in the country of departure might include outbound passenger lists, visa or passport applications, or police emigrant records.

UK Outbound Passenger Lists 1890–1960
(www.ancestorsonboard.com)

The UK National Archives in association with Findmypast .com has created a searchable database featuring passenger lists for long-distance ships departing the British Isles between 1890 and 1960. Images of the passenger lists are available to download, view, save, and print. Searching is free; transcriptions and images of the passenger lists are available on a pay-per-view basis.

Hamburg Passenger Lists 1850–1934
(www.ancestry.com)

Between 1850 and 1939, Hamburg, Germany, served as the "Gateway to the World" for about 5 million European emigrants. An index to the existing Hamburg lists from 1890 to 1912 was initially created and placed online by the Hamburg State Archives, but was later moved to the subscription-based site Ancestry.com. Ancestry's immigration collection also includes digitized copies of the passenger lists for ships that departed from Hamburg from 1850 to 1934 (with a gap from 1915 to 1919 due to World War I).

Bremen Passenger Lists 1920–1939
(www.passengerlists.de)

The majority of the passenger lists from the port of Bremen, Germany, were lost during World War II. This database offers access to the 3,017 passenger records that survived.

Danish Emigration Database (www.emiarch.dk)

Emigration lists compiled by the Copenhagen Police from 1869 to 1908 have been transcribed and included in this free, searchable database. Information includes the name, last residence, age, year of emigration, and first destination of the emigrant from Denmark.

Norwegian Emigration Lists
(*http://digitalarkivet.uib.no*)

Click on English and then Database Selector to find data on emigrants that National Archives of Norway extracted from ships' lists, police emigration records, and other sources, including digital images. Norway Heritage (*www.norwayheritage.com*) is another excellent source for information on emigrants from Norway.

Border-Crossing Records—Canada and Mexico

Keeping records on alien arrivals at U.S. land borders was not required by early immigration acts. It wasn't until 1895 for Canada and about 1906 for Mexico that immigration authorities began to collect information on immigrants arriving in this manner. Separate card manifests were created for each individual that contain virtually the same information as that collected on a traditional ship passenger arrival manifest. These border-crossing records have been microfilmed and can be requested through any Family History Center. Online, Ancestry.com has an index and images of the records of aliens and citizens crossing into the United States from Canada via various ports of entry along the U.S.-Canadian border between 1895 and 1956.

Critical Clicks

No discussion of immigration research on the web is complete without mentioning Steve Morse and his one-step search tools. These search forms (*www.stevemorse.org*) provide powerful interfaces for searching popular existing genealogical databases, including major immigration and naturalization databases such as Ellis Island, Castle Garden, and the immigration databases at Ancestry.com.

The National Archives and Records Administration is currently processing microfilmed immigration records for individuals who crossed the U.S.-Mexican border between about 1903 and 1955 at land border ports in Arizona, California, New Mexico, and

Texas. These are available for research through National Archives locations. Digital images of these records, along with a searchable index, are available online to subscribers at Ancestry.com.

Naturalization Records

Naturalization is the legal procedure by which an alien becomes a citizen of a country. Every nation has different rules that govern these requirements for citizenship. The records generated by the naturalization process can help you learn key information about your immigrant ancestor, including the place of birth and date, ship, and port of arrival. How much you can learn, however, will depend upon when and where the naturalization took place.

Congress passed the first law regulating naturalization in 1790. As a general rule, naturalization was a three-step process that took several years and generated a number of different documents:

1. First, the prospective citizen filed a declaration of intent, also referred to as first papers, to become a U.S. citizen, in which she renounced allegiance to foreign sovereignties. This document was signed by the immigrant.
2. Following a prescribed waiting period—generally two to five years—the immigrant could petition a federal court for formal citizenship. This did not have to occur in the same court in which she filed her declaration of intent. The application completed by the individual in this step is called the petition for naturalization.
3. After the petition was granted, a formal certificate of citizenship was issued to the petitioner.

Typically, the declaration provides more genealogically useful information than the petition. Prior to September 26, 1906, the declaration generally includes the name, country (but not town) of birth or allegiance, the date of the application, and the signature (if the individual being naturalized could write). Many included additional information, but the content varied dramatically from county to county, state to state, and year to year. Naturalizations after September 26, 1906, were handled on standardized forms, and include more detailed information such as the town of birth and the port and date of arrival.

As you can see, September 26, 1906, is a key date for naturalization research. Copies of all naturalizations after that date were forwarded to the newly formed U.S. Bureau of Naturalization for examination and are presently in the custody of U.S. Citizenship and Immigration Services (*www.uscis.gov*), which makes them easy to locate when you don't know where your ancestor was naturalized. Those more than fifty years old can be ordered online through the USCIS Genealogy Service (select "Genealogy" from the Other Services section of the left-hand navigation menu). These naturalization certificate files, known as C-files, generally contain a copy of the declaration of intent (to 1952), the petition for naturalization, and the certificate of naturalization. Occasionally, C-files also contain additional documents or correspondence.

Prior to September 26, 1906, an alien could be naturalized in any court of record—including courts at the local, county, state, or federal level—and the naturalization documents are usually found maintained among the court's records. Often it was a matter of the alien choosing to travel to the most conveniently located court with the authority to naturalize, so you may want to begin your search by identifying the courts closest to the place your ancestor lived at the approximate time she was naturalized.

Remember, the approximate year of naturalization can be found on the 1920 census if your ancestor was living at that time.

Some naturalization indexes and records can be found online. Fold3.com is an excellent source, with digitized indexes and naturalization records for several U.S. states including Maryland, Massachusetts, Pennsylvania, New York, and (Southern) California. Ancestry.com has many digitized naturalization records as well. For naturalization records found on various archives and personal sites, Joe Beine comes to the rescue with his list of Online Searchable Naturalization Indexes and Records (*www.germanroots.com/naturalization.html*).

Were They Eligible, or an Exception?

During certain points in American history, a variety of men, women, and children either were eligible to skip a few steps in the naturalization process or were granted automatic citizenship based on eligibility. Minor children, for example, were automatically granted citizenship upon the naturalization of their father. For a time (1855 to 1922), a woman could also achieve automatic citizenship either by marrying a citizen or upon the naturalization of her husband. Conversely, between 1907 and 1922, a female American citizen could lose her citizenship by marrying a man who was a foreign national, even if she never left the United States. From 1824 to 1906, minors who had lived in the United States at least five years before their twenty-third birthday (including those whose parents were not naturalized) were able to skip the declaration step, as were individuals who served in the U.S. armies (Union forces) during the Civil War.

Racial requirements also affected eligibility for naturalization as a U.S. citizen. The naturalization process was first opened to people of African descent on July 14, 1870. Native Americans born outside the United States were barred from citizenship on racial grounds until 1940. The Chinese were the first Asians to gain the right to naturalization, in 1943; most had to wait until 1952, when the racial requirement was stricken from U.S. immigration law.

Not All Aliens Were Naturalized

Aliens living in the United States were not required to become citizens and, during the nineteenth century, citizenship really gained them little other than the right to vote. Alien residents could legally buy and sell property, hold a job, and get married without citizenship status. For this reason, many nineteenth and early-twentieth-century immigrants—at least 25 percent according to answers recorded in the 1890 through 1930 censuses—lived most of their lives in the United States as aliens and either never began or never completed the process of naturalization.

If census or other records lead you to believe that your ancestor never pursued naturalization, don't despair. Alien registration and visa records are often similarly rich in genealogical details. Information was collected on noncitizen residents of the United States at various points during American history, including special wartime registrations of alien citizens of "enemy" countries and a nationwide registration effort in the 1940s. Beginning in 1924, aliens arriving in the United States were required to apply for immigrant visas, which offer yet another source for information on foreign-born residents.

The Immigration Act of 1924 prompted a major change in U.S. immigration. Beginning July 1 of that year, everyone arriving at a U.S. port of entry was required to present some type of entry document. This might include a birth record or naturalization certificate for U.S. citizens, a re-entry permit for alien residents of the United States, or an immigrant visa or other paperwork for noncitizens. Prospective immigrants wishing to settle in the United States were required to apply for an immigrant visa at a U.S. embassy abroad. Those traveling to the United States for a temporary purpose, such as a visit or to attend school, applied for a nonimmigrant visa.

Fears of unknown enemies living within the United States prompted registration of resident aliens during wartime. These enemy alien registration records covered aliens who were living in the United States and were citizens of a country against which the United States had declared war.

The first such large-scale effort was prompted by World War I, when from November 1917 to April 1918 all resident, non-naturalized "enemy" aliens, including their American-born wives, if applicable, were required to register with the U.S. Marshal in their county of residence as a national security measure. These alien registration forms documented citizens of the German empire living in the United States, including the date and ship of arrival, children's names and birth dates, parents' names and address, whether the alien was sympathetic to the enemy, names of relatives serving in the enemy forces, occupation and employer, a physical description, and a photograph and full set of fingerprints.

The majority of the World War I enemy alien records were destroyed in the 1920s by authority of Congress, but state and/ or local copies of records for Kansas, Minnesota, Missouri, and the Phoenix, Arizona, area, as well as a few scattered other registrations, still survive. Selected records can be found online.

The Alien Registration Act of 1940 required all alien residents age fourteen and older to register with the U.S. government and be fingerprinted. Aliens entering the country registered as they applied for admission. This alien registration requirement applied to all aliens over the age of fourteen, regardless of their nationality and immigration status. Millions of the aliens who registered had already lived in the United States for many years.

Alien registrations completed between July 1940 and April 1944 were microfilmed and placed in the custody of U.S. Citizenship and Immigration Services. These records are searchable by name, date of birth, and place of birth, and copies may be obtained through the USCIS Genealogy Program.

Ethnic Research

Ethnic heritage is more than just a source of pride. It also offers alternative research strategies and resources for tracing your family tree. Different ethnic groups, both in the United States and abroad, preserve and maintain a variety of records of interest to genealogists. If you take time to become familiar with and explore these resources, you may learn something new about your own family heritage.

A variety of societies and organizations have been formed to collect, disseminate, and preserve the records and heritage of specific ethnic groups. These groups can often point you to specific records of interest for researching your ethnic ancestors. To locate such societies, look through the comprehensive directory of the Federation of Genealogical Societies Society Hall (*www.fgs.org/cstm_societyHall.php*).

Whether you're researching African American, French-Canadian, Jewish, Irish, Hispanic, or Native American ancestry, a variety of specialized databases relating to most ethnic or religious groups can be found online. Excellent examples include AfriGeneas (*www.afrigeneas.org*) for African American research and JewishGen (*www.jewishgen.org*) for individuals tracing their Jewish heritage. The National Archives maintains an excellent list of links to major websites for ethnic genealogy research (*www.archives.gov/genealogy/heritage*), as does Cyndi's List (*www.cyndislist.com/topical.htm*—look under Ethnic Groups and People).

CHAPTER 10

Locate Records Abroad

Now that you know how to find information about your immigrant ancestors, you'll need to begin searching for those they left behind when they came to America (parents, grandparents, siblings, etc.). Since 95 percent of Americans today have descended from individuals who did not live on this continent in the eighteenth century, it probably won't be long before your research leads you past America's borders.

If you're worried that you don't have the skill for foreign research, don't be. The research skills and techniques that you already use readily transfer to research in a new location. Yes, there will be a few stumbling blocks, such as language barriers. You'll also need to spend time familiarizing yourself with the country's history, including changing political and geographical boundaries. But once you find that first ancestor in the "old country," you'll be hooked!

Limited space prevents going into extensive detail on genealogy research in every country around the world. Instead, this chapter takes a look at some of the major online family history resources available for a variety of countries, with links to websites where you can access further research guidance and resources on the countries where your ancestors may have lived.

Canada

A large amount of genealogical and historical data for Canada is already available online, with more being added all the time. Most records are maintained at the province level, so you will need to have an idea of what part of Canada your ancestors came from before embarking on your research.

> **Where can I find Canadian records of birth, marriage, and death?**
> Civil registration of vital statistics in Canada is a provincial responsibility; available records and access will vary by province. Some archives and vital statistic offices, such as the British Columbia Archives, offer online indexes to historical birth, marriage, and death registrations. Others only provide information on how to order a certificate via mail. Try a search such as "Canada vital records" or "Alberta vital records" or "Ontario marriages" to learn what's available in your area of interest.

Billing itself as a "gateway to Canadian genealogy," the CanadaGenWeb Project (*www.rootsweb.com/~canwgw*) is available in English and French with queries, lookups, and a FAQ. Besides links to province-specific resources, you'll discover a timeline of Canadian history, facts about famous Canadians, a cemetery transcription project, and a special website just for kids.

The Canadian Genealogy Centre (*www.collectionscanada .gc.ca/genealogy/index-e.html*) of Library and Archives Canada has posted numerous (and free) online databases that are useful for anyone researching Canadian roots. Select Search for Ancestors to find the 1851, 1901, and 1911 censuses of Canada; a variety of immigration records and passenger lists; naturalization records; land grants; and early marriage bonds for Upper and Lower Canada.

If you are having trouble locating your ancestor in the Canadian census images on the Library and Archives Canada site, head on over to Automated Genealogy (*www.automatedgenealogy.com*). Several genealogy projects are under development at this free, volunteer-supported website, including indexes of the 1901, 1906, and 1911 censuses of Canada.

A growing collection of Canadian family history records is available for free online access at FamilySearch.org. Select "All Collections" from the main page at FamilySearch.org and then narrow by location to Canada to view available records such as the 1851, 1871, and 1891 census indexes, plus index and images for the 1881 Canadian census. FamilySearch also has 1861 census returns for Quebec, Nova Scotia, New Brunswick, Ontario, and Prince Edward Island, plus a large number of vital records, both national and provincial.

The largest collection of Canadian family history records available online can be found on the subscription site Ancestry .ca (*www.ancestry.ca*).

The fully searchable databases include indexes and images for the 1851 through 1916 censuses of Canada, along with Canadian immigrant records and vital records from most provinces. Other interesting Canadian collections include the Canada Militia and Defence Forces Lists, 1863–1939, plus the historic Drouin collection, with more than 37 million baptism, marriage, and burial records. This is a companion site to the U.S.-based Ancestry.com and includes the same records, although a Canada Deluxe membership that only includes Canadian records is available exclusively on Ancestry.ca.

Find information on more than 116,000 Canadians and Newfoundlanders who fought and died while in service to Canada at the Canadian Virtual War Memorial (*www.vac-acc.gc.ca/remembers/sub.cfm?source=collections/virtualmem*). Information in this free database includes the individual's military service number, unit and division, date of birth, and burial information. It also often includes that individual's hometown and the names of spouse and parents.

Since many of Canada's records are created and maintained at the provincial level, you'll want to check the archives, libraries, and other repositories in the province where your ancestors lived. The site That's My Family (*www.thatsmyfamily.info*) helps make this easy, offering a free online search interface for multiple databases from various provinces. Canadian Genealogy and History Links (*www.islandnet.com/~cghl/*) is an excellent resource for web links to provincial archives and libraries, as well as other resources for Canadian genealogy. You can also find a wealth of Canadian research guides and database links at Cyndi's List—Canada (*www.cyndislist.com/canada.htm*) and About.com Genealogy—Canada (*http://genealogy.about.com/od/canada*).

Mexico, Central America, and South America

The countries of Central and South America do not yet have many family history records available online. The free FamilySearch site (*www.familysearch.org*) is quickly changing that, however. You can also use the Internet to learn how to conduct research in these countries, and find contact information and instructions for ordering records.

Find Births and Marriages at FamilySearch

Available for free searching via the FamilySearch website (*www.familysearch.org*), the Mexico vital records indexes include more than 44 million baptism, 6 million marriage, and almost 400,000 death records from Mexico, a partial listing of records covering the years 1560 to 1950. It also contains 1930 Mexico Census and Mexican civil registration records and Catholic Church records. FamilySearch has census and/or vital records collections for many Central and South American countries as well, including Argentina, Brazil, Costa Rica, the Dominican

Republic, Ecuador, El Salvador, Grenada, Guatemala, Honduras, Jamaica, Panama, Paraguay, Peru, and Uruguay. From the FamilySearch home page, scroll down and select a country of interest to begin navigating your way to available records.

> **Critical Clicks**
> Before you dig into the online databases, it pays to become familiar with the ins and outs of genealogy research in your country of interest. Introductory guides to research in many countries around the world can be found at FamilySearch.org (*www.familysearch.org*). Select "Learn" from the top navigation bar and then search or browse for your country of interest.

Locate Country-Specific Resources at GenWeb

Visit the North America Genealogy Project (*www .worldgenweb.org/index.php/northamgenweb*) to locate online resources and records, and to connect with fellow researchers for the countries of Central America, including Belize, Costa Rica, El Salvador, Guatemala, Honduras, Nicaragua, and Panama. For genealogy research in South America—encompassing the countries of Argentina, Brazil, Colombia, Chile, Peru, Venezuela, and others—the South AmericanGenWeb Project (*www.worldgenweb.org/southamericangenweb*) serves as an online repository for source records, family histories, genealogy queries, and links to online databases.

Both sites are free and fully supported by volunteers.

The British Isles

There is a vast wealth of data available for the regions that make up the British Isles—England, Scotland, Wales, Ireland, the Channel Islands, and the Isle of Man. There is, in fact, much more than can be adequately discussed in this book. But to get you started, two of the best jumping-off points include GENUKI and the BritishIslesGenWeb. GENUKI (*www.genuki.org.uk*), short for GENealogy of the United Kingdom and Ireland, serves as a virtual reference library of genealogical information with relevance to the United Kingdom and Ireland. It's a great place to look for links to vital websites and primary source documents organized by region, county, and topic. The BritishIslesGenWeb site (*www.britishislesgenweb.org*) has genealogical data and queries, along with links to the eleven British Isles country projects (Caribbean Islands, Channel Islands, England, Falkland Islands, Gibraltar, Ireland, Isle of Man, Northern Ireland, Scotland, St. Helena, and Wales). Don't miss their Location Finder—a useful tool for identifying the location of your ancestor's parish.

Once you've spent some time exploring the records available at the volunteer projects discussed in this chapter, it's time to jump into online records and databases.

Census Records

Like census records in the United States, censuses in most of the British Isles were conducted every ten years—but in the second year of the decade (the years ending in "1") instead of the first. Because they cover the entire population, they are among the most comprehensive records available online for research in this region.

The free records at FamilySearch (*www.familysearch.org*) are a good place to begin your census research with complete indexes to the 1841, 1861, and 1881 England and Wales Census. From there, make a stop at FreeCEN (*www.freecen.org.uk*), where volunteers worldwide are transcribing UK census records for 1841, 1851, 1861, 1871, and 1891. Coverage varies widely—with some counties and years almost 100 percent complete, and other counties with nothing. GENUKI, as well as Census Online (discussed in Chapter 5), are good places to find links to free census indexes, transcriptions, and images organized by region and county.

Once you've exhausted the free offerings, censuses from 1841 through 1911 (the most recent released to the public) can be viewed on a variety of pay-per-view or subscription sites. Ancestry.com offers census indexes and images for all years in England, Wales, Scotland, the Channel Islands, and the Isle of Man as part of their World Records Collection subscription. The National Archives offers free online searches of the 1901 census of England and Wales (*www.1901censusonline.com*), although you'll have to pay to access full transcriptions and digital images. The official genealogy website of the Scottish government, ScotlandsPeople (*www.scotlandspeople .gov.uk*), offers subscription-based access to indexes and images of the Scottish census, for the years from 1841 to 1871 and 1891 to 1901, plus index and transcription (no images) of the 1881 census. FindMyPast (*www.findmypast.com*) offers a free census search and your choice of pay-as-you-go or subscription access to census transcriptions and images for the complete census of England and Wales, 1841 through 1911. The Genealogist (*www.thegenealogist .co.uk*) offers inexpensive subscription access to transcripts, indexes, and images for the England and Wales census 1841 through 1901. Another alternative for the 1841 census, which has a more accurate index than other offerings, is available at subscription-based BritishOrigins (*www.origins.net*).

Census records for Ireland are not quite as easy to come by. The 1861, 1871, 1881, and 1891 census enumerations were destroyed by government order during World War I. The 1901 and 1911 Ireland census records, however, have been digitized and made available for free online use by the National Archives of Ireland (*www .census.nationalarchives.ie*). In the absence of earlier Irish census records, Griffith's Valuation of Ireland 1847–1862 can be searched online at the Origins Network (*www.origins.net*). Named for its director, Richard Griffith, Griffith's Valuation was an evaluation of every property in Ireland, conducted between the years 1847 and 1862. It doesn't offer details on family members as census records do, but does provide a listing of the owner and occupier of each piece of property.

Critical Clicks

The volunteer indexing project at the Genealogist offers rewards in the form of vouchers and subscriptions in return for time spent assisting in their transcription efforts. As a volunteer, you would participate in error-checking previously indexed entries, using special online tools. If you have some free time to offer and would enjoy free database access in return, consider signing up as a volunteer at UKIndexer (www.ukindexer.co.uk).

Civil Registration Records—Births, Marriages, and Deaths

Online access to vital records in the British Isles is a breath of fresh air after the inconsistent availability of such records in the United States. In addition, all British Isles civil registration records are open to the public, including even the recent records. England and Wales share the same civil registration system, while Scotland, the Republic of Ireland, and Northern Ireland each have separate systems.

Civil registration in England and Wales was instituted nationwide on July 1, 1837. Searching these records is much easier than the painstaking state-by-state process most American genealogists are used to, because the General Register Office (GRO) maintains a national index of these births, deaths, and marriages. The alphabetical index, arranged first by year and then by quarter (March, June, September, and December), includes the surname, first name, registration district, and volume and page of the GRO reference. The mother's maiden name was added to the birth index in 1911 and the spouse's name to the marriage index in 1912. Online access to the GRO or BMD (birth, marriage, death) index is available from the following sites:

- FreeBMD (*http://freebmd.rootsweb.com*)—This massive volunteer project aims at creating a full transcription of the GRO BMD indexes for England and Wales. As its name implies, the database offers free access. The primary focus of FreeBMD is the period from 1837 to 1903, although many more recent records are available. Work is ongoing, and the project does not yet include the entire index. A copy of the FreeBMD database is also available for free searching on Ancestry.com, the project's financial supporter. Both sites offer the same data, although FreeBMD offers links to the original index images; response times can sometimes be faster on Ancestry.com.

- BMD Index (*www.bmdindex.co.uk*)—This pay-as-you-go subscription site features the complete BMD index in the form of digital images from the original record books. It also offers full name searching and better bang for your buck than other subscription-based sites. Searches only point you to the pages in each quarter where your ancestor's name might appear. You'll still have to view the actual pages—at least one for each quarter per year—to locate them in the index.

- FindMyPast (*www.findmypast.com*)—Previously mentioned for its census records, FindMyPast offers pay-per-view access to digitized images of all original GRO index pages from 1837 to 2002. It offers a surname-only search to help narrow down the pages you need to view.

When searching for marriages in the BMD Index, there's a technique you can use to identify the spouse in the pre-1912 marriage indexes. In the FreeBMD index, all you have to do is click on the hyperlinked reference link to view the other names appearing on the same page. If you already know the spouse's name, finding his or her name on that page will help you confirm that you have found the correct index reference. If you don't know the spouse's name, you can use this to help narrow down the potential candidates. When viewing actual index images, you'll need to search the pages for both surnames (look for the more uncommon one first) to see if they appear on the same reference page. This, of course, means you'll need to know at least the spouse's last name. Of course, by ordering a copy of the actual marriage certificate, you'll be able to confirm the names of both parties in the marriage.

Once you've located the reference to your ancestor's birth, death, or marriage from the GRO index, you can easily order a copy of the original certificate online through the GRO's certificate-ordering service (*www.gro.gov.uk/gro/content/certificates*). Online fees for this service are comparable to what you would pay in person at the Family Records Centre in London or through the local register office. You'll need a valid credit or debit card to use this service.

Civil registration in Scotland began on January 1, 1855, and returns are kept at the New Register House in Edinburgh. The previously discussed ScotlandsPeople website (*www .scotlandspeople.gov.uk*) offers an index and online images of the original registers of births more than 100 years old, marriage records more than 75 years old, and records of deaths more than 50 years old. The best part about this service is that you don't have to wait for the certificate to arrive—you can view digitized versions of the actual handwritten register images online. Certificates of more recent births, marriages, and deaths have to be ordered directly from the General Register Office of Scotland (GROS) (*www.gro-scotland.gov.uk*). Disappointingly, this site doesn't yet offer online ordering, but it does include directions for ordering a certificate in person, by mail, or by telephone. For free research in Scotland's civil registration records, the International Genealogical Index (IGI) at FamilySearch, previously discussed in the book, includes entries from the first twenty years of births and marriages recorded under Scottish civil registration (1855 to

1875). If you do find your ancestor in this database, you may want to confirm the entry by ordering a copy of the actual certificate.

Official registration of births, marriages, and deaths in Ireland began in 1864, although state registration of marriages for non–Roman Catholics began earlier, in 1845. The civil registration index is arranged alphabetically by year until 1877, after which each year was divided into quarters as in England and Wales. FamilySearch .org (*www.familysearch.org*) offers free online access to the civil registration indexes for Ireland from the beginning of registration to 1958. Certificate copies can be ordered online through the General Register Office of Ireland (*www.groireland.ie*).

Emerald Ancestors (*www.emeraldancestors.com*) offers a variety of vital records databases containing extracts and records from civil registrations for Counties Antrim, Armagh, Down, Fermanagh, Londonderry, and Tyrone. Monthly and annual subscription-based access is available.

What is the best website for researching Scottish ancestors?
A first stop for anyone researching Scottish ancestry should be ScotlandsPeople (*www.scotlandspeople.gov.uk*), the official family history website of the government of Scotland. It offers a wealth of genealogical data on a pay-per-view system, including indexes and registers of civil births, marriages, and deaths from 1855; records of births, christenings, and marriages appearing in parish registers from 1553 to 1854; census records from 1841 to 1901; and wills and testaments from 1513 to 1901.

Births, Marriages, and Deaths in Parish Records

Before the recording of births, marriages, and deaths in the British Isles became a civil issue, such vital events were recorded by individual parishes in the form of baptisms, marriages, banns, and funerals. The earliest date you'll generally find such parish registers in England and Wales is 1538, although many churches did not begin keeping records until 1558 or later.

The recording of parish registers in Scotland, Ireland, and the rest of the British Isles began around the same time. After 1598 in England and Wales, a copy of the prior year's register for each parish was also forwarded to the bishop of the diocese. Known as Bishops' transcripts, these copies provide a second record of the valuable parish registers, and may have survived when the parish register has not.

The FreeREG site (*http://freereg.rootsweb.com*), a companion to the previously discussed FreeCEN and FreeBMD, offers free Internet access to baptism, marriage, and burial records that have been transcribed by volunteers from parish and nonconformist registers of the United Kingdom. Another free alternative for parish records is the International Genealogical Index (IGI) at FamilySearch, which includes information collected and transcribed from parish registers from the British Isles by the Church of Jesus Christ of Latter-day Saints. Both sources offer a good avenue for locating information from parish registers online, but because they are transcriptions you may want to check the information you find against the original parish register (or a microfilm or digital copy of the original) to verify that it has been accurately transcribed. Subscription-based access to many UK parish registers is available through Ancestry.com and FindMyPast.com. FamilySearch (*www.familysearch.org*) is also continuously adding new free collections of online parish registers and Bishops' transcripts for England, Scotland, Wales, and Ireland.

In addition to the previously mentioned census and civil registration records, ScotlandsPeople also offers access to births, baptisms, banns, and marriages from old parish registers of Scotland from 1553 to 1854. The Emerald Ancestors site, previously discussed for Irish vital records, offers entries from a selection of parish registers for the period 1796 to 1924.

France

The French approach family history with a passion, which you'll soon find evident as you start to familiarize yourself with the many available genealogy projects and databases for this country. The records are fairly well preserved, despite several wars and much social upheaval, and date back well into the sixteenth century. The biggest drawback to French genealogy on the Internet is that most of the databases, records, and websites are only available in French. Don't let this scare you away, however. With a good French genealogy word list and the help of online translation tools you'll soon be able to navigate your way around French records.

You'll also want to familiarize yourself with the geopolitical divisions in France. Instead of counties, you'll find France broken up into *régions* (similar to our states) and *départements* (similar to our counties). Within each département, you'll find cities, towns, and villages, called *les mairies*. Archives are generally found at the département level, while local records are maintained by each parish and mairie. Départements in France are each assigned a number, so you'll need to learn both the name and number of the département to access appropriate records.

A good place to begin your research into French ancestry is GeneaNet (*www.geneanet.org*), a genealogy community for publishing and sharing family trees, connecting with other researchers, and locating records. While the site operates as a worldwide genealogy database, the primary focus is still on French ancestry. Because the site is available in English and several other languages in addition to French, it offers an easy introduction to French genealogy research. Search by surname and/or village to help locate databases that may contain information on your family, and to connect with other genealogists who are researching your surname.

Another good gateway site to French genealogy is the FranceGenWeb (*www.francegenweb.org*) portal. Much of the site is presented in French, although some portions can also be found in English. Use FranceGenWeb as a gateway to find online databases and records, connect with fellow researchers, and locate the départemental GenWeb sites. The Historical Databases at FamilySearch.org also include a number of offerings for France, from births, baptisms, and marriages to Protestant church records.

Critical Clicks

Many départemental archives in France have digitized civil, parish, and census records and have made them available online for free viewing. The Archives of France website (*www.archivesdefrance.culture.gouv.fr/ressources/en-ligne*) maintains a comprehensive and up-to-date listing of available online records by department.

When it comes to records of interest to family historians, France boasts an excellent system of civil registration records dating back to September 1792. Prior to that time, Catholic parish registers (*registres paroissiaux*) record baptisms, marriages, and funerals in much of France. The earliest parish registers date back to 1334, although the majority of surviving records date from the mid-1600s. These civil and parish records are being made available online, primarily on the websites of the various départemental archives, at a rapid rate. The French census, conducted once every five years beginning in 1836, is another useful record for researching French ancestors. These census records aren't indexed, which makes it hard to locate your ancestors in larger cities, but with patience they can provide you with a great deal of information about your family. Check the website of the départemental archive to see if they offer digitized images of their census records (*recensements de population*).

Italy

There is no central repository for most Italian genealogical records, so the first step in researching Italian ancestors is to identify the town (*comune*) or municipality (*municipio*) where they lived. Civil registration was instituted in Italy in 1804, although the Napoleonic-era records are very inconsistent. Once Italy became unified as a country in 1860, civil registration again became a priority of the Italian government. The majority of these records of birth (*atti di nascita*), marriage (*atti di matrimonio*), and death (*atti di morte*) begin in 1866 and continue to the present day. As in France, the predominant religion of Italy is Roman Catholic, so Catholic parish records provide another excellent resources for vital records—baptisms (*atti di battesimo*), and burials (*atti di sepoltura*). The majority dates back to 1563, although some church records begin as early as the 1300s.

There are not a lot of records for Italy available online. You can find transcriptions of selected Italian civil records at Transcribed Vital Records of Italian Towns (*www.sersale.org/comunes.htm*). As with other countries around the world, Italy GenWeb (*www.italywgw.org*) offers a good resource for Italian genealogy, with online archives and records, how-to guides, and contact information for fellow researchers. Once again, FamilySearch (*www.familysearch.org*) is leading the pack, with more than a million combined birth, baptism, marriage, and burial records from Italy, plus civil and municipal records, plus Catholic Church records.

Scandinavia

The Scandinavian countries of Norway, Sweden, Denmark, Finland, and Iceland offer a wider variety of online genealogical records than most people expect. As with most European countries, the key to Scandinavian genealogy is in knowing the name of your ancestor's hometown or parish. This region's GenWeb sites, accessed through CenEuroGenWeb (*www.rootsweb.com/~ceneurgw*), offer good introductory information on the available records of interest to genealogists, as well as forums for connecting with other researchers.

A good online source for Scandinavian vital records is the free FamilySearch historical records collection. Click on All Collections from the main FamilySearch page (*www.familysearch .org*), and then Europe in the left-hand navigation bar to access vital records from Scandinavian countries such as Norway and Iceland.

The Norwegian Historical Data Centre at the University of Tromsø (*www.rhd.uit.no/indexeng.html*) is working to computerize many of the historical records of Norway. The site offers free access to the complete Norwegian census of 1865 and 1900, and digitization of the 1875 census is under way. This source also offers access to selected parish registers and other genealogical sources from the eighteenth and nineteenth centuries.

In Sweden, the best site for online genealogy research is Genline (*www.genline.com*), where you can access digitized images of original Swedish parish registers on a subscription basis. The site is available in English, so you can easily identify which parish registers are available before plunking down money for a subscription. You can also buy a twenty-four-hour demo subscription for a reasonable price.

Swedish church records are also available online, again for a fee, from the Swedish National Archives (*www.svar.ra.se*). This site also offers the complete 1880, 1890, and 1900 censuses of Sweden, plus death records and other databases of interest. Look for a link at the top of the home page to an English version of the site.

The online database of the DIS Computer Genealogy Society of Sweden (*www.dis.se*) contains more than 22.2 million records of Swedes born before 1905 submitted by members. Searches of this database are free, but only members can access the full details. This site also offers an English-language version.

In Denmark, the Danish State Archives (*www.sa.dk*) features a number of online databases including a probate index, some census records, and the Danish Demographic Database (*www .ddd.dda.dk/ddd_en.htm*). Look for an English link on the site home page. The site also includes a link to the Danish Emigration Archives (*www.emiarch.dk*), where you can search a database of emigration lists compiled by the Copenhagen Police from 1869 to 1940 (the database only includes the years up to 1908). These lists give the last name, last residence, age, year of emigration, and first destination of almost 400,000 emigrants from Denmark. Don't miss the linked collection of online church books (*www .sa.dk/ao/Kirkeboeger/default.aspx*).

As you might expect in such a remote country, almost every member of the 300,000 population of Iceland is related to one another. Islendingabok (*www.islendingabok.is*), meaning "Book of Icelanders," is a database that includes Icelandic family trees and genealogies going back for more than 400 years, covering the roughly 720,000 individuals who were born in Iceland at some point in time. Unfortunately, only Icelanders are allowed access to this database.

Germany

Many genealogists believe that it can be harder to trace your roots in Germany than in any other European country because of changing boundaries and the destruction of records during the two world wars. Germany as it is known today wasn't even established until 1870, and German descent is no guarantee that your roots reach back to Germany at all. Instead you may find them in Poland, Ukraine, the Czech Republic, Slovakia, Russia, Hungary, Yugoslavia, or Lithuania. Even small portions of Belgium, Denmark, and France were obtained from German territory in 1919.

> ### Critical Clicks
> *Germans to America*, edited by Ira Glazier and P. William Filby, is a sixty-seven-volume set of books indexing German arrivals to America between 1850 and 1897. A second series covers the 1840s. This series can be found at many major libraries—a partial list of libraries that have them can be found on Genealogy.net (*www.genealogienetz.de/misc/emig/gta-holdings.html*).

That being said, there are several good sources of German genealogical information available online. Genealogy.net (*www.genealogienetz.de*) sponsors a variety of mailing lists, lists German genealogical societies, and links to a number of helpful databases. Some portions of the site are only available in German. Bremen Passenger Lists (*www.schifflisten.de*) offers a searchable database of passenger departure records from Bremen for the years 1920 to 1939. All surviving records from this time period—2,851 out of 4,420 lists—have been transcribed and made available online by the genealogical society, Die Maus.

For further research links to German genealogy on the Internet, check out the GermanRoots website (*www.germanroots.com*) maintained by genealogist Joe Beine. It includes a comprehensive list of links to online genealogy records, books, and other resources, as well as a basic research guide for German genealogy.

Eastern and Central Europe

For most of the remaining European countries, access to online records is a bit limited. The Internet still comes in handy for research in the countries of Eastern and Central Europe, however. Online you can find a wealth of information on the changing political and geographical boundaries of the region, as well as maps, historical documents, and opportunities for connecting with other people researching your surnames.

Begin your search at the site of the Federation of East European Family History Societies (FEEFHS) (*www.feefhs.org*), which is geared toward assisting North Americans in tracing their ancestry back to a European homeland. The site offers links to participating member societies, maps, and helpful online databases for research in Eastern Europe. It also includes a useful collection of ethnic, religious, and national cross-indexes. Another excellent starting point is the EastEuropeGenWeb Project (*www.rootsweb.ancestry .com/~easeurgw*) where you can access queries, family histories, and source records, as well as connect to the country GenWeb sites, from Albania to Yugoslavia. For the countries of Central Europe, you'll find many of the same resources at CenEuroGenWeb (*www.rootsweb.ancestry.com/~ceneurgw*).

If you have the name of the town or village in Central or Eastern Europe where your ancestors originated, ShtetlSeeker (*http://www.jewishgen.org/Communities/LocTown.asp*) can help you determine its present-day location.

Moving on to country-specific databases and resources, the Polish Records Transcription Project (*www.rootsweb.com/~polwgw/ transcribe.html*) at PolandGenWeb offers access to birth, marriage, and death records for many towns in Poland. The PolandGenWeb archives also include links to transcriptions of a few Polish cemeteries and other helpful information. Additional records for Polish genealogy research, including maps, gazetteers, obituary

indexes, and cemetery listings, can be accessed at PolishRoots (*www*
.polishroots.com). While there, check out the popular SurnameSearch
registry, where you can register the surname you are researching and
access a variety of surname databases.

For individuals with roots in what was Czechoslovakia prior
to 1993 and is now Slovakia or the Czech Republic, It's All
Relative (*www.iarelative.com*) includes a great deal of information
on surnames, places, and databases to help you search your
Czech, Bohemian, Moravian, Slovak, Lemko, or Carpatho-
Rusyn family history. Other helpful sites for this area of Eastern
Europe include the Carpatho-Rusyn Genealogy website (*www*
.rusyn.com), The Carpathian Connection (*www.tccweb.org*), and
Cyndi's List (*www.cyndislist.com/czech.htm*), which offers links to
hundreds of additional resources for researching ancestors from
the Czech Republic and Slovakia.

A collection of several hundred small databases and records
useful for researching ancestry in the Eastern and Central
European countries of Austria, Hungary, Poland, Russia, Slovakia,
and Ukraine is available for searching at the subscription-based
WorldVitalRecords (*www.worldvitalrecords.com*) site. There are
also hundreds of thousands of free genealogy records available for
Eastern and Central European countries online at Family Search,
including vital and other records from the Czech Republic,
Germany, Hungary, Russia, Austria, Slovakia, and Ukraine.

Swiss family history is best begun at Swiss Genealogy on
the Internet (*www.swissgenealogie.ch*) where you can find an
introduction to researching Swiss ancestors, the Register of Swiss
Surnames, and links to websites about Swiss families. Another
useful site is Swiss Roots (*www.swissroots.org*), which serves as
a gateway for Americans of Swiss descent looking to discover
their ancestors. Here you can access a small handful of useful
databases, learn a little about Swiss history and culture, and read
about some famous Americans of Swiss descent.

Australia and New Zealand

Like the United States, Australia and New Zealand are fairly young countries where the majority of the population is only a few generations removed from its immigrant roots. Government-created records are scattered and inconsistent, and many have limited access because of very restrictive privacy laws.

Records of birth, marriage, and death in Australia and New Zealand are maintained at the state or territory level. A good listing of the BMD Registrars, along with links to the registrars that offer free or fee-based online access to Australian birth, death, and marriage indexes can be found at Cora Num's excellent website for genealogists (*www.coraweb.com.au/bdmaut .htm*). This gateway site also includes well-researched links to archives, cemeteries, census records, convict records, and passenger lists for Australia. Once again, FamilySearch has a nice collection of free records for Australia and New Zealand, including births, baptisms, marriages, deaths, and burials, plus immigration passenger lists and Masonic records. Subscription-based site Ancestry.com also includes Australian vital records, plus electoral rolls, lists of assisted and unassisted immigrants, cemetery records, and much more.

In New Zealand, registration of European births and deaths was first required in 1848, and marriage records from 1854. Registration of Maori births and deaths did not become compulsory until 1913, under a separate system of registration that applied to individuals of half or more Maori blood. The older New Zealand historical records (*www.bdmonline.dia.govt .nz*), not protected by law, can be ordered online by anyone for a fee.

The National Library of Australia in Canberra has a special section devoted to Australian family history (*www.nla.gov.au/ oz/genelist.html*), with links to state libraries and genealogical societies as well as several databases for online research. These include immigration, military, and convict records.

Many people with Australian ancestry hope to discover a convict in their family tree. To this end, Convicts to Australia (*www.convictcentral.com*) includes a research guide, timeline, lists of the convict transport ships, convict databases, and stories of convict ancestors.

> **Genealogical Guidance**
> Maori are the indigenous people of New Zealand. It is believed that the Maori originally emigrated from Polynesia in canoes about the ninth century to thirteenth century A.D. There are currently a little more than 400,000 Maori living in New Zealand, comprising about 13 to 14 percent of the country's total population.

Asia and Africa

The large and diverse continents of Africa and Asia present a challenge for anyone attempting to research African or Asian family history. Very few records are available online. The Internet can still provide a great research tool for learning about the history of the area where your ancestors once lived and for connecting to other genealogists with research interests in the area.

AfriGeneas (*www.afrigeneas.com*) is the largest jumping-off point for Americans looking to trace their roots back to Africa, with records, forums, and mailing lists devoted to helping you connect your African American ancestors to their place of origin in Africa. Once you have at least identified your ancestor's country of origin in Africa, the AfricaGenWeb Project (*www.africagenweb.org*) may provide some assistance with directing your research efforts in Africa. If your ancestors were from South Africa, spend some time exploring the National Archives of South Africa (*www.national.archives.gov.za*), where you can search an index to several helpful databases. It is important to note that these are only indexes to available records. The actual documents will need to be requested from the Archives.

The AsiaGenWeb Project (*www.worldgenweb.org/index.php/asiagenweb*) includes links to a variety of country websites, covering a broad area from Turkmenistan in the west to East Timor in the east. Many of these sites are actually in need of hosts, and thus provide little in the way of useful information. The best include ChinaGenWeb (*www.rootsweb.ancestry.com/~chnwgw*) and JapanGenWeb (*www.rootsweb.ancestry.com/~jpnwgw*). For people tracing European ancestry in India, the Families in British India Society (*www.fibis.org*) provides a number of useful lists and databases. An interesting site for those with Korean ancestry is the Korean History Project (*www.koreanhistoryproject.org*). Yes, FamilySearch (*www.familysearch.org*) has some historical records online too, including vital records for India, Sri Lanka, and the Philippines.

CHAPTER 11

Connect with Other Genealogists

Discovering your roots can be a very personal journey, but it isn't something you'll easily accomplish alone. This is where the Internet truly offers an advantage for family history research, allowing you to easily connect and collaborate with other researchers. You can learn from and exchange data with others looking for similar information, discover previously unknown relatives, benefit from the experience and knowledge of others, or get help from individuals with access to records in far-off places. It's also really nice just to interact with other genealogists who share the same passion for family history that you do!

Make the Most of Boards and Lists

One of the easiest ways to connect with other researchers who may have information on your family is through genealogy-specific message boards and mailing lists. They serve as a prominent means of communication among family historians on the Internet and allow for a tremendous amount of research sharing. Best of all, they're free and convenient. Most even allow you to search through archived postings, and some offer e-mail notification when a new query is posted that matches your surname or region of interest.

Join a Genealogy Mailing List

You can learn a lot by joining a mailing list focused on the surname, topic, or region on which your research is focused.

Subscribing is as simple as sending an e-mail to the list administrator. Once you've joined, you'll receive copies of all e-mails sent to the list by other subscribing members and can send your own messages, which will be received by everyone on the list.

Most genealogy mailing lists offer two subscription modes:

- List mode—You'll receive each message posted to the mailing list individually as it is sent (or after it is approved by the list moderator).
- Digest mode—You'll receive periodic e-mails (usually daily) with several mailing list messages appended together. This can be a great method for reducing clutter in your inbox, but this mode can make it harder to follow a specific conversation.

After you subscribe, you'll usually receive a welcome e-mail within a few hours. Be sure to save this e-mail, as it will generally include important information on list rules and how to unsubscribe.

No matter what your genealogy research interest, there is probably a mailing list that applies—from individual surnames (such as CRISP) to research in specific counties or areas (such as the very active Bristol_ and_Somerset-L mailing list at RootsWeb) or topics that you might want to stay on top of (such as genealogy DNA). The vast majority of genealogy-related mailing lists (more than 30,000) are hosted through RootsWeb (*http://lists.rootsweb.ancestry.com/*) on topics such as surnames and places, immigration, religion, prisons, and heraldry. Check out Gen-Newbie for beginner-level help on anything from research to software. If you're a more advanced researcher, there are plenty of options for you as well, including the *Advanced Research and Transitional Genealogists Forum* lists. Alternatively, you can use your favorite search engine to search for a mailing list on a particular topic, such as "genealogy 'mailing list' 'pitt county' nc."

Genealogical Guidance

Genealogy mailing lists are similar to a community or neighborhood in that they reflect the personalities of their subscribers. Some lists are friendly with a number of off-topic "chatty" posts, while others are more strictly moderated with no off-topic discussion allowed. When you first join a mailing list it is a good idea to "lurk" for a few days to get a feel for the list and its members before posting your first message.

Delve Into Genealogy Message Boards

Genealogy message boards and forums are different from mailing lists because messages are posted online, rather than sent to your e-mail address. Some message boards are open for anyone to browse and post to, while others require you to join for full access. As with mailing lists, they are free. The downside is that you have to remember to visit the message board periodically to find new messages, but most boards will at least send you an e-mail notification when someone responds to one of your postings and some will let you know whenever a new message is posted that matches your surname or area of interest. The upside is that message board postings will not clutter up your inbox like mailing lists do, so if you're short on time, message boards may be a good option for you. Because message board posts are archived online, most show up in Internet search engines. This increases the chances that your query for information on your great-grandfather Charlie just might be found by someone with some answers.

Genealogy message boards and forums can be found in many locations online. The largest, most frequented boards are those at GenForum (*www.genforum.com*) and Ancestry.com (*http://boards.ancestry.com*). Although not a true message board, CousinConnect (*www.cousinconnect.com*) is another popular place for connecting with other researchers. It is dedicated solely to genealogical queries, and responses are sent directly to your e-mail. RootsChat (*www.rootschat.com*) is a popular genealogy messaging forum focused on Ireland and the British Isles.

> **Critical Clicks**
>
> Newsgroups, such as Yahoo! Groups (*http://groups.yahoo.com*) and Google Groups (*http://groups.google.com*), are similar to message boards, but they also incorporate the e-mail feature of mailing lists. In short, you get to choose whether you want new messages sent to you via e-mail or if you prefer to only read the new messages online. Many genealogical societies and genealogy research lists can be found on these sites.

Search the Archives

Message boards also allow you to search or browse through past posts, providing an excellent tool for connecting with other researchers. The RootsWeb mailing lists are archived online as well (*http://archiver.rootsweb.com*), going all the way back to the beginning of the first genealogy mailing list, Roots-L, in 1987. Visit message boards and archived mailing lists for your primary surnames of interest and try searching for given names or locations from your family tree. Don't forget to search beyond the immediate family for spouses, cousins, siblings, and even neighbors. It's possible that people searching for those individuals may have information about your direct ancestors as well.

If you find a message you're interested in, even if it is an old one, take the time to reply with a brief message about the individual(s) you are researching and how you think they connect. This not only leaves a trail for the individual who originally posted the message, but may also catch the attention of others researching the same family. For tips on posting your own genealogy queries on message boards and mailing lists, see the "Ask the Right Way" section later in this chapter.

Search for Family Trees

You probably wouldn't believe the number of people who think that genealogy is nothing more than a hunt for an already completed family tree. Since you're reading this book, you probably already realize that it doesn't work that way. But with millions of people becoming involved in researching their family history, large numbers of family trees are available on the Internet, and your chances of locating at least a portion of your family tree online are better than you might think.

Find Family Trees at FamilySearch

The FamilySearch website currently offers a single family tree search engine that draws from more than 4.1 billion names contained in three different family tree databases of information culled from pedigree charts and family trees submitted to the Family History Department of the Church of Jesus Christ of Latter-day Saints (LDS).

- The International Genealogical Index (IGI) is a database of more than 285 million baptisms and marriages from around the world, along with a few births and burials. Many of these events were extracted from original records, while others were submitted by members of the LDS Church. Click on the Source Call No. link from the IGI individual record page to learn the source of any data you find.
- Ancestral File is a lineage-linked database that includes family trees submitted by family historians worldwide, created primarily from submissions gathered since 1979. Duplicate individuals from various contributors have been merged (not always correctly) and the only source information generally available for these trees, if any, is the name of the submitter.

- Pedigree Resource File was created to overcome some of the deficiencies of Ancestral File, and includes notes and sources when provided by the contributor. These family trees are generally more recent, submitted by users to the FamilySearch Internet service. Only the index to the Pedigree Resource File can be searched online, however. For full access to a particular GEDCOM file, including source citations, you'll need to purchase the CD on which the GEDCOM is published. These are sold at cost, generally in sets of five, and can be purchased online.

The new FamilySearch Family Tree (expected to debut to the public on FamilySearch.org sometime in 2011) will also feature user-submitted family trees via a more user-friendly pedigree interface. The goal, according to FamilySearch, is to eventually create a single lineage-linked tree.

How reliable is the information found in online family trees? Many of the family trees submitted online are works in progress, and most probably contain at least an error or two. For this reason, you should never just download a family file you find online and add it directly to your own research without first taking some time to assess the accuracy of the information.

Member Trees at Ancestry.com

From the Ancestry home page (*www.ancestry.com*), click on the Family Trees tab to search for your ancestors in family trees submitted by members. (If you don't see a Family Trees tab, begin by clicking on Search in the navigation bar at the top, and then select Family Trees.) Search results will turn up family trees in a number of different collections, although Member Trees is their most current offering, with more than 1.8 billion names contained in 18 million–plus user-submitted family trees. You can also submit to and search family trees through the free WorldConnect website (*http://worldconnect.rootsweb.com*) at RootsWeb.

GenCircles Global Tree

This is another popular database of lineage-linked family trees, contributed by users to the site (*www.gencircles.com*). Everyone can search and view the trees for free, but if you submit your own GEDCOM file to GenCircles you can also take advantage of its SmartMatching technology to pair the people in your family tree file with other family trees in the database.

Take Your Search Global at GeneaNet.org

This pedigree database boasts more international family trees than most, and can be accessed in many languages as well. Because it was founded in France, GeneaNet (*www.geneanet.org*) is especially useful for searching family trees from France and other countries of continental Europe. There is a cost to upgrade to a Privilege Club membership, which offers enhanced search options and other features, but the family trees can all be searched and accessed free of charge. A handy e-mail alert can even notify you when new trees are added that match your criteria.

Search the Social Networks

Social networking sites offer yet another opportunity for connecting with others who may also be researching your ancestors. Facebook is one of the biggest these days, with several genealogy applications such as FamilyLink's We're Related (*www.facebook.com/myrelatives*) and FamilyBuilder's Family Tree (*http://apps.facebook.com/familytree*) available to help you add your family tree to your Facebook profile. You'll need a little patience, however. Those Facebook apps aren't the easiest to use. Facebook also has hundreds of genealogists talking back and forth to each other every day, plus pages for dozens of genealogy groups and family history societies. In addition, there are also quite a few social networks dedicated primarily to family history and related topics.

MyHeritage (*www.myheritage.com*), available in fifteen languages, is the largest and most widely used, with free online software for building your family tree and smart matching technology to help you connect with others who may be researching the same relatives. This site also offers a free mobile app so you can stay on top of your search wherever you are. Dozens of similar sites exist online, including Family Link (*www.familylink.com*), and Genes Reunited (*www.genesreunited.co.uk*). Most, though not all, of the genealogy-related social networking sites are free, although you'll often have to sign up as a member to search the family trees of other members.

Find Family Trees by Subscription

Genealogy is big business, and many companies make money by collecting and distributing family trees submitted by users. Genealogy.com, for example, offers WorldFamilyTree, a collection of family trees submitted by users of Family Tree Maker software and/or Genealogy.com. You can search these family trees online for free in Genealogy.com's Family Finder, but the family files (which include contact information for the contributor) are only available through online subscription to the website or for purchase on CD-ROMs.

Ancestry.com offers free online searching of their online Member Trees, and even nonpaying members who have been invited to view a tree are allowed to also view the attached records, assuming that the tree owner is a paying subscriber. Public Member Trees can be viewed by all Ancestry subscribers, while Personal Member Trees present only limited information online. Instead, you'll be offered the chance to connect with the person who submitted the family tree for further details through

the Ancestry Connection Service. You'll need a free Ancestry
.com guest account to use Member Trees.

In addition to the sites discussed here, there are dozens of
other lineage-linked family tree databases to be found online, as
well as thousands of individually created family trees published
on personal websites across the Internet. Many can be found
by entering a search such as "Bumgardner family tree" in your
favorite search engine.

> **Genealogical Guidance**
> In order to read and follow many of the family trees you'll find published
> online, it will help to have a basic understanding of the conventional
> numbering systems used by genealogists. Three of the most common
> include the Ahnentafel, a numbering system for ascending genealogies,
> and the Register System and NGS Quarterly System, used for descending
> genealogies. Examples and explanations of each system can be found
> online through a Google search.

Ask the Right Way

As you search the web, you'll eventually come across other individuals researching the same ancestors. They may have information on your family that has been passed down to them,
including treasured photographs, family stories, or even official
documents and records. Or they may have researched a family
line that you haven't yet had the time or resources to pursue. The
first instinct—and generally a good one—is to contact them via
e-mail. Keep in mind, however, that while your shared interest
in the same ancestors means they are likely to be related to you
in some distant way, in reality these people are basically strang-
ers to you, as you are to them. To better ensure that your e-mail
is opened and answered, or your message board post isn't overlooked, consider the following:

- Include a meaningful subject line. An e-mail from an unknown sender with a subject line of "Help!" is likely to be deleted without being read. Include the surname or full name of the individual you are writing about, as well as something like "genealogy" or "family history." Subject lines such as "Powell Genealogy" or "Family Tree of Archibald Powell" are more likely to catch someone's attention than "Hi."
- Keep it simple. Explain briefly who you are and how you received the individual's name and e-mail address, as well as how you are related to the family you are contacting the person about. Consider this first e-mail as an introduction to test the waters. It's not the best time to share your entire life story.
- Be precise. Many people throughout time have shared the same name, so you'll need to include additional details to help people identify the individual you're interested in. Where did he live? About when was he born? Can you provide names of other members of his family? Briefly explain what you already know or where you've already searched for this individual.
- Don't ask for the moon. A genealogist who has been patiently researching their family for years isn't really going to appreciate an e-mail asking for "everything you have on my family." Most genealogists are exceedingly generous in sharing the information they have uncovered, but be reasonable in what you ask for. Asking for a few specific facts, such as a marriage date or parents' names, is a good rule of thumb. They may offer to share more, of course, but they'll appreciate that you don't expect it of them.
- Protect the privacy of the living. While it's okay to share the names of your living relatives with other people, please don't give people their birth dates, social security numbers, or other private information.
- Offer to share information in return. If you're asking for something specific, it generally pays to offer something in

return. Perhaps you have some old family photos, documents, or dates that this individual may be interested in.

- Say thank you. Take a few minutes to respond with a quick note of thanks for any information or response you receive, whether it is truly helpful to you or not.

These guidelines also apply to posting queries about your family online, whether on a genealogy forum or through a mailing list. Keep your query short and sweet, but include a relevant subject line, identifying details about your ancestor, and an overview of the places you've already searched.

Volunteer help can also be of tremendous assistance when researching your family tree. The genealogical community tends to be a very generous, giving group of individuals. All you have to do is ask a question and you'll usually get an answer. Help can be found almost anywhere you look, but Books We Own (*www.rootsweb.com/~bwo*) is especially notable for the volunteer assistance it provides. This free service has been around for more than a decade, connecting volunteers who own or have access to genealogy-related books and other published resources with people who need a quick lookup for their ancestor or a specific surname.

Share Your Research

You can drastically improve your chances of connecting with other people researching your family line by making it easier for them to find you. Many people have connected with other branches of their family tree through an online website or community forum. Even the information posted through online obituary services and remembrance books has been known to bring families together.

One of the easiest ways to share your family history online is to upload a GEDCOM of your family history file to one or more of the lineage-linked databases previously discussed in this chapter. Your family tree doesn't need to be "finished" or even close to it, as long as what you do contribute has been well researched and you're comfortable with its accuracy. If your family tree is still very much a work in progress and you are unsure of some of your information, look for a service that allows you to easily add information or make corrections as your research progresses.

When creating your GEDCOM file for online publication, consider how much information you want to share online, and what you hope to achieve.

- It's always a good idea, of course, to remove personal information about living individuals before publishing your family tree online.
- Many people choose to include their sources, as this makes it easier for others to follow your research. Some family historians worry, however, that if they provide too much information people will just take and add it to their own family tree without contacting the researcher, which works against the point of putting the family tree online in the first place. To avoid this, some researchers choose to eliminate their sources from online family trees, and instead include a note asking anyone who is interested in further information to contact the researcher.
- If you like to use the Notes field of your genealogy software for everything from contact information to personal thoughts, stories, and questions concerning your relatives, it is best to leave that on your computer and not make it part of your online family tree. That generally falls under the category of "too much information."

If you don't feel comfortable sharing your entire family tree online, there are other good options for reaching online researchers. One good way to connect with others who may be researching your family is to add your surnames to the RootsWeb Surname List (*http://rsl.rootsweb.ancestry.com/*), a free service that exists for the sole purpose of bringing researchers together. More than 1 million surnames are listed here, along with associated dates and locations where they are being researched. Each posting also includes the e-mail address of the person who submitted the surname so you can contact him or her directly. You can (and should) also post the surnames, dates, and locations that you're researching to the appropriate genealogy mailing lists and message boards discussed earlier in this chapter.

If you're creative and want to go beyond what most family tree databases offer, you may want to consider publishing your own family history website or blog. Publishing your family history online in this manner is discussed in more detail in Chapter 12.

Connect with the Pros

As much fun as it can be to research your own family history, there can be times when it pays to turn to a professional for help. Maybe you just don't have the time to really dig into the records, or need some experienced assistance with putting all the pieces together. Or you might want to hire someone to do record look-ups in a faraway city, or to take all of the bits and pieces of your research and turn them into a beautifully written family history. Sometimes you just need inside knowledge of local records, or a little extra help with a very stubborn problem.

Aren't genealogy conferences only for professionals?
Contrary to popular belief, genealogy conferences and institutes offer all genealogists—from the beginning hobbyist to the advanced professional— the opportunity to learn something new. They also offer the opportunity to learn from some of the world's best genealogists, keep up with new techniques and methodologies, and sample the latest software and gadgets. You can even take a genealogy cruise!

Join a Society

Some organizations, such as lineage societies, genealogical societies, and patriotic organizations, focus primarily on preserving the genealogy and family history of their members and/or region and making it available to the world. By joining such a society, you not only enjoy extra access to its records but can also benefit from the experience of the members. Most societies publish newsletters and quarterlies with record transcriptions, genealogy queries, articles on available records and resources, and news of interest to researchers. Many also offer some type of free or reduced-cost research benefits to their members, as well as the opportunity to include personal queries in their publications. Societies also generally arrange a variety of workshops, seminars, and research trips for their members. And, of course, there is the wonderful opportunity to network with other society members.

But what if the bulk of your research is not in your hometown? Do you join your local society? Or the society covering the area in which your ancestors lived? Both situations have their benefits. Many genealogists choose to belong to their local genealogical society, despite having no ancestors from the area, for the chance to actively participate in the local genealogical community, in addition to joining societies in the areas where their ancestors lived. While you may not be able to attend the meetings or actively participate in the business of societies outside your area, membership still affords you the ability to keep up with the latest research news and resources through newsletters and quarterly publications. Many societies also operate mailing lists, so you can participate to an extent without leaving home.

Even if you choose not to join a genealogical society, most offer benefits to nonmembers as well. This often includes access to their library collection and a system for requesting research, lookups, and/or copies. Historical and genealogical societies are also good places to turn for inside information on records and repositories that will aid you in your research and for answers to your local research questions. They may have a website with searchable records, a forum for posting queries, or a mailing list that offers the opportunity to ask questions, request a lookup, or share the details of your family.

To find a genealogical or historical society near you, or that meets your research interests, visit the Society Hall (*www.fgs.org/cstm_societyHall.php*) operated by the Federation of Genealogical Societies. This site offers contact information on more than 500 societies throughout the United States. Cyndi's List (*www.cyndislist.com/society.htm*) has several thousand links to societies and groups, organized alphabetically by the name of the society rather than geographically. You can also easily find many societies by entering a search such as "Pennsylvania genealogical society" or "mennonite genealogy society" in your favorite search engine. Check out your favorite genealogical societies on Facebook as well! Thomas MacEntee maintains a good list of Facebook—Genealogy Society Pages (*www.hidefgen.com/facebook-genealogy/facebook-genealogy-society-pages*) to get you started.

Network with Other Genealogists

As mentioned previously, genealogists are connecting on a regular basis on Facebook as well as through Twitter, mailing lists, study groups, and other networking opportunities. This gives you the option to ask questions of other genealogists at all stages of research, as well as the many genealogists in the process of transitioning to professional careers in genealogy. Here are just a few examples of the many ways genealogists are using the Internet to learn from one another and make new friends.

- Facebook (*www.facebook.com*)—If you have a Facebook account, or choose to create one, you can instantly find a few hundred genealogy "friends" to hang out with online. Here's a Partial List of Genealogists on Facebook (*www.hidefgen.com/facebook-genealogy/facebook-genealogy-society-pages*) to get you started from Thomas MacEntee. It's great when you attend your first genealogy conference and already feel like you know everyone from Facebook!
- Twitter (*www.twitter.com*)—Twitter is more than just a place to tell people what you ate for breakfast. Genealogists are using it as a means to meet and learn from others who share their interest. It's a great place to learn about upcoming genealogy events or sales, get opinions on genealogy websites or products, ask questions, or just learn from (or laugh at) what other genealogists are talking about. The Twitter Cheat Sheet from GeneaBloggers (*www.geneabloggers.com/twitter-cheat-sheet*) will get you started.
- ProGen Study Group (*www.progenstudy.org*)—Organized study groups for aspiring professional genealogists that employ collaborative learning focused on developing genealogical skills and best business practices.

Hire a Professional

To locate a reputable genealogist for your project, it is best to turn to a professional association. These groups work to ensure quality and ethics among professional genealogists, which can offer you a certain element of confidence in the person you are hiring. Two organizations within the United States provide credentials or certification to genealogists from around the world who have passed rigorous tests of their research skills. The Board for Certification of Genealogists (BCG) (*www .bcgcertification.org*) offers research credentials as a Certified Genealogist (CG), as well as in a supplemental teaching category, Certified Genealogical Lecturer (CGL). A second credentialing organization, the International Commission for the Accreditation of Professional Genealogists (ICAPGen), also offers testing of genealogists worldwide through comprehensive written and oral examinations. It offers the designation of Accredited Genealogist (AG). The Association of Professional Genealogists (*www .apgen.org*) is another good place to turn when looking to hire a professional. This umbrella organization is not a credentialing body, but instead works to support high standards in the field of genealogy and requires all of its members to adhere to a code of ethics.

Critical Clicks

Expert Connect at Ancestry.com (*http://expertconnect.ancestry.com*) is a platform for bringing professional genealogists together with the individuals who need their services. Invite experts to bid on your project, whether it's document translation or a custom research project, and then select the expert who best meets your needs.

All three groups offer an online member list or database to assist you in locating a researcher by geographical location or specialty. Should you be dissatisfied with the work done by a member, each group also offers arbitration or other options to help in rectifying the situation.

CHAPTER 12

Putting It All Together

Now that you have learned the basic research steps, processes, and sources used in tracing your family tree, it is time to put everything you have learned into practice—to evaluate what you have uncovered and assemble it into a well-researched family tree; to publish or otherwise share your family history with others; and to protect your family's heritage from possible loss or disaster.

Evaluate What You've Found

Just as with a puzzle, each piece, or fact, that you uncover about your ancestors needs to be evaluated to determine its appropriate placement in the family tree. What is the record telling you? Is the information complete? How convincing is it? Does it conflict with other information that you've found?

What Does the Document Say?

Reading old records is something you'll have to do often as you trace your family tree back in time. Handwriting styles were definitely different, and the writers weren't always very particular about punctuation and penmanship. Words may have had different meanings, and even dates weren't always as self-explanatory as you might think. An important step in evaluating the information you've found is to make sure that you've interpreted it correctly.

Even modern handwriting can be difficult for genealogists to read because of poor penmanship. As you go back in time, the difficulties only increase as you encounter unusual scripts and other handwriting oddities along with archaic spellings and usage. You don't have to be an expert in paleography to accurately read old documents, but some practice and experience is a must. Online tutorials can be extremely helpful in this regard. On About.com Genealogy, the Photo Glossary of Old Handwriting and Script (*http://genealogy.about.com/od/ paleography/ig/old_handwriting*) includes alphabets and example text for some of the most common handwriting scripts used prior to the twentieth century. Easy-to-use tips and examples are included in *"Deciphering Old Handwriting"* (*www.amberskyline .com/treasuremaps/oldhand.html*) by Sabina Murray. For help learning to read documents written in British English between 1500 and 1800, the UK National Archives offers an outstanding practical online tutorial in paleography (*www.nationalarchives .gov.uk/palaeography*).

Dates in genealogy documents can cause confusion as well. A date in a marriage index may be the date that the marriage license was issued or the banns were announced, not the actual date of marriage. Along the same line, people often confuse the dates for births and baptisms, and deaths and burials. Be sure to pair up the date with the correct event.

Once you go back far enough in your family tree, you may encounter different calendar systems, including the Julian calendar, French Republican calendar, various religious calendars, and the unusual Quaker system of dating. You may also find archaic usage relating to dates that you may not recognize. The term *instant*, for example, refers to the month, as in "the eighth instant." The corresponding term, *ultimo*, refers to the previous month. Examples of other archaic date usage you may encounter include Tuesday last, referring to the most recent Tuesday, and

Thursday next, meaning the next Thursday to occur. Dates were sometimes recorded based on their relationship to another event, as well. A common example of this practice is regnal years, where the year is recorded by the number of years since the accession of the reigning monarch (e.g., 2008 is the fifty-fifth year of Elizabeth II's reign).

Sometimes genealogy seems to have a language all its own. As you dig into older records you'll come across unfamiliar terms and puzzling abbreviations. It is important that you look up the correct interpretation of such terms as you encounter them so that you don't miss any important clues. Latin terms are the most commonly encountered in genealogical documents, from the legal language of wills and deeds to the Latin records of the Roman Catholic church. The abbreviation et ux., for example, is one that you'll commonly encounter, from the Latin words *et uxor*, meaning "and spouse." Most of these words can be easily looked up online; check out the extensive Latin genealogical word list at FamilySearch (*http://wiki.familysearch.org/en/Latin_ Genealogical_Word_ List*) or consult a Latin-English dictionary. Other archaic and obsolete terms, such as those commonly used to describe occupations and medical conditions, can also be looked up online. Try a Google search for the unrecognized term, or browse through the variety of online specialized dictionaries created for this purpose (search for old occupations or archaic medical terms to find such dictionaries and glossaries).

Genealogical Guidance

In 1582, Pope Gregory XIII ordered that ten days be dropped from the Julian calendar that was in effect at the time, and that the beginning of the year change from March 25 to January 1. This new system was the Gregorian calendar still in use today. Because of this calendar change, you may encounter events recorded with a double date, such as 20 March 1718/1719.

Prove Your Argument

Proof in genealogy is very rarely an absolute. The facts that you uncover about your family tree may be used as evidence to support your conclusions, but you can really only call it proof if you and others find it convincing. A census record that lists your great-grandma living on her own as a widow certainly provides evidence that her husband is deceased. It isn't proof, however. The census enumerator may have made a mistake in entering the information, or the woman may have stated that she was a widow for any number of personal reasons. The evidence is there, but it isn't convincing enough to be considered proof when evaluated on its own.

So what constitutes proof? Genealogists define proof as a combination of the evidence and reasoning that convincingly supports a conclusion. Evidence alone doesn't constitute proof. A single document can, on occasion, offer enough evidence to present a reasonable conclusion. Yet, the proof exists not only in the document itself, but also in the fact that other reasonable sources were searched and no conflicting evidence was found.

You'll often encounter situations in your research where several elements of direct evidence conflict with each other. On the other hand, there will also be circumstances where no individual piece of evidence explicitly provides the information you seek. In these cases, the "proof" comes from analyzing each piece of evidence and creating a logical argument as to why the information, when taken together, carries enough weight to support your conclusion. This is a proof argument, a detailed discussion of the problem, the evidence for and/or against your conclusion, and the resolution of the problem. To assist genealogists in determining whether their evidence and reasoning is sufficient to support their conclusions, the Board for Certification of Genealogists has defined a series of five elements that need to be met before a conclusion can be considered satisfactorily credible or "proven." Known collectively as the "Genealogical Proof Standard," the five criteria are:

1. Reasonably exhaustive search for a wide range of high-quality sources
2. Complete and accurate citation of sources
3. Analysis and correlation of the collected information
4. Resolution of any conflicting evidence
5. Soundly reasoned, coherently written conclusion

A genealogical conclusion that meets this standard of proof can be considered convincing or "proved." This still doesn't imply that your conclusion is true or absolute, just that it is the most logical given the presented evidence.

I'm just doing this for my family. Why all the fuss over sources and evidence?
What difference does it make whether Great-Grandma died in Georgia or Alabama? Or where the birth date for Grandpa came from? Like anything else, family history is really only worth doing if you're interested in doing it well. The best way to honor your ancestors is to represent them correctly and take pride in your work.

You Can't Find Them! Now What?

In the process of researching your family history, you'll likely encounter research problems that just don't seem to have a solution. Perhaps your ancestor has a common name, making it impossible to sort him out from all the other men by that name that appear in the records. Maybe your ancestors pulled a disappearing act between the 1880 and 1900 U.S. census. Or maybe you have followed your ancestors back to the point at which they "crossed the pond," only to have their trail sink into the Atlantic. What's the next step?

- Retrace your steps. Review the information you have already collected. You've probably learned many new things since you first started tracing your family tree, and the information may reveal new facts when you look at it with fresh eyes. There may be names that had no significance when you first encountered them, or you may be able to better read the old handwriting now that you've had some practice. New sources also come online every day, so take time to retrace some of your Internet searches and revisit your favorite database sites to see what's new.

- Check your facts. Are you looking for the right name? In the right place? For the right person? Many brick walls are built from incorrect assumptions. If you have used a lot of compiled databases or published sources to construct your family tree, go back and check them against original documents. If your ancestors lived near a county line, check the neighboring county for records. Investigate all potential name variations for your ancestor as well—not just various spellings of the surname, but given-name alternatives including initials, middle names, and nicknames.

- Branch out sideways. The cluster genealogy technique introduced back in Chapter 2 really comes in handy when your research hits a dead end. This is especially true in cases where ancestors seem to have disappeared. Because family, neighbors, and friends often moved together, you may find a clue to their former home or their new location by tracing the movements of the people with whom your ancestors had a connection. When you can't find an ancestor in a particular census, for example, conduct a search for their neighbors from the previous or succeeding census. This technique also works well for passenger lists.

- Don't do *all* of your research online. For every genealogical record and source available online, there are hundreds more tucked away in archives, libraries, courthouses, and other offline repositories. The Internet is very valuable as a research tool, especially for the survey phase, but you can't use it as your only resource in a thorough family history search. Use online catalogs and other resources discussed throughout this book to become familiar with other potential sources of information about your family located offline, and then visit or write to the repository or hire a researcher to do it for you.

One of the best ways to learn successful genealogical research methods is by reading and studying published case studies. These real-life examples are written by genealogists to describe a particular research process, and the method by which they arrived at their conclusions. Many explore particularly knotty or confusing research situations, so they can be full of creative searching ideas. Numerous genealogical case studies and articles online even specifically offer advice on getting past genealogical brick walls. Michael John Neill has written two articles that may help inspire your creativity, titled "Brick Walls from A to Z" (*www .rootdig.com/adn/brickwall_a_z.html*) and "More Brick Walls, A to Z" (*www.ancestry.com/learn/library/ article.aspx?article=11723*). In addition, his article listings at Rootdig.com (*www.rootdig.com/ adn*) include quite a few case studies and other real-life examples of working through apparent research dead ends. At About.com Genealogy you'll find "Brick Wall Strategies for Tracing Dead-End Family Trees" (*http://genealogy.about.com/od/basics/a/brick_ walls.htm*), as well as several case studies (*http://genealogy.about .com/od/case_studies*).

Protect Your Family History from Disaster

If you had to evacuate your house and only had minutes to get out, what would you take? The boxes of photos in the back of your bedroom closet? The photo albums on the coffee table in your family room? The computer in your study? The genealogy files in your basement? In a disaster situation you often won't have time to grab much, and generally won't have time to go looking. You may not even be home when disaster strikes, which leaves you no time at all. Important pieces of your family history, even those that had survived for centuries, could be gone in an instant.

Back Up Your Computer Files

In the age of the Internet people have come to rely on their computers for everything from online banking to digital photo storage. The downside of this reliance on technology, however, is that catastrophes such as fire, theft, computer viruses, and hardware failure can cause you to lose years of hard work or irreplaceable memories in an instant. Don't make the mistake of believing that it won't happen to you. It happens more often than you might think. But the results don't have to be catastrophic if you back up your genealogy files and digital documents on a regular basis.

There are a wide variety of backup options available, and with technology changing constantly it's probably best to explore these online. Consider using USB flash drives, and external hard drives.

Online backup services offer another easy method for backing up your precious computer files and digital photos. You can store your data offline, away from your home where a disaster might strike both your computer and your backups at once, and use automatic scheduling of backups so there is no more forgetting to back up your files. Cost is a factor in such services, however. ConsumerSearch recommends the best online backup services (*www.consumersearch.com/www/internet/online-backup-services*) based on their appraisal and rating of a number of online reviews.

Duplicate and Distribute

Sharing your family history like this is one of the best ways to assure that nothing important is ever lost. Make copies of precious photos and documents and mail them off to family members. Send relatives a GEDCOM of your family tree file. Create a genealogy website for disseminating your research. Upload your photos to an online photo-sharing service. All of these steps take a little time, but will ultimately safeguard your family history from potential disaster. Your family members will appreciate the gifts as well!

Don't Overlook the Hidden Dangers

Light, temperature, moisture, pollutants, and the odd bug or two all threaten the survival of family heritage. The solution doesn't have to be complicated, however. Basically, it's a matter of making the time to transfer your photos, documents, wedding dress, family Bible, and other family heirlooms into archival-safe boxes, albums, and storage containers. Once they're appropriately packed, they just need a safe home. Find a spot in your house that maintains normal indoor temperature year-round and is generally dark and dust free, such as a closet shelf, a storage trunk, or even under the bed. If you're in a flood-prone area, keep things above known flood levels. You should almost always avoid the attic, basement, and garage because they tend to experience large variations in temperature and/or moisture.

Information and supplies for proper storage and preservation of family photographs and documents are easy to locate online. Experts at the National Archives answer questions on storing photographic prints, when to remove photos from an old album, and how to safely attach photos or memorabilia to album or scrapbook pages on their Caring for Your Family Archives web page (*www.archives .gov/preservation/family-archives*). Archivist Sally Jacobs offers ongoing practical tips for genealogists and others interested in preserving their family's heritage on her entertaining blog, the Practical Archivist (*http://practicalarchivist.com*).

Publish Your Family history

One of the joys of researching your family history is sharing the results. Family trees can be displayed and presented in a wide variety of ways. A beautiful framed chart can be hung on your wall or presented as a gift. The stories of your ancestors can come to life through a published family history book. Old family photos can take on new life as a scrapbook. Your family history can reach a wide audience through a genealogy website or blog.

Write It Down

A written family history can be as short and simple or as long and detailed as you want. To most family members, it will be priceless, regardless of the size or complexity. The first step is to decide what you want your family history to be. Will you begin with an ancestral couple and document all of their descendants, or work your way back up your own direct line? How many generations will your family history cover? Will you include family photographs? Who will buy your book, or whom do you plan to share it with?

Once you've decided on some of the basics, the Internet offers a wide range of resources to assist you with your project. GenWriters (*www.genwriters.com/write.html*) has pulled many of these together in one place, with links to a variety of how-to articles and tips, plus a bibliography of family history writing guides.

If you don't want to do the writing or layout yourself, you can hire an individual or company to prepare your family history for you. Search for family history publishers or genealogy book printers to find companies that can help you with your project. If you're looking for someone to actually write the book for you, the member directory of the Association of Professional Genealogists (*www.apgen.org*) includes listings for quite a few genealogists who specialize in this area.

Share Your Family History Online

Probably the easiest way to share your family history online is to publish your pedigree to one of the popular online pedigree databases such as RootsWeb WorldConnect (*http://worldconnect.rootsweb.com*), Ancestry Member Trees (*http://trees.ancestry.com*), FamilySearch Family Tree (*www.familysearch.org*), or GenCircles (*www.gencircles.com*). All you have to do to use these free services is to upload a GEDCOM file from your family tree program and they turn the information into a series of online searchable pedigrees. This solution allows your family tree to be found by people searching the Internet, yet requires very little work or technical knowledge.

Another easy option for sharing your family history online is to create a page on a site that offers a set of easy tools for putting your family tree online. The popular social networking site Geni (*www.geni.com*) is one such example. This site took off quickly after its launch early in 2007, attracting more than 5 million users in just five short months who share everything from family trees to a family calendar, messaging, and photo sharing. Geni isn't the only social networking site on the Internet working to attract family historians, however. Others, such as WeRelate (*www.werelate.org*), MyHeritage (*www.myheritage.com/family-tree*), and GeneaNet (*www.geneanet.org*) let you build an online family tree, collaborate with your family members, connect with other researchers, and share photos and recipes. Many offer secure, password-protected sites if you want to keep your family history in the family.

If you want a little more custom control over the layout, content, and design of your site, you may want to create a full-blown genealogy website. There are free hosting options, such as the popular FreePages (*http://freepages.rootsweb.com*) at RootsWeb, and TribalPages (*www.tribalpages.com*). Alternatively, you can purchase space and even your own domain name through any hosting service. Many family tree software programs include nice online publishing features to make sure the process of getting your actual pedigree online is done in a nice, browsable format. For step-by-step guidance, check out the NGS guide, *Planting Your Family Tree Online: How to Create Your Own Family History Website*, by Cyndi Howells.

You may also want to try blogging your family history. A blog, short for web log, is basically a type of online journal with text, photos, and other goodies. You don't need to know any HTML or programming to use blogging software, and you can use it through a free online hosting service such as WordPress (*www.wordpress.com*) or Blogger (*www.blogger.com*). You can also, if you choose, install the software on your own website. A blog varies from a traditional genealogy site by having each entry dated, like a journal, and therefore people expect them to be updated frequently. This makes them a perfect medium for sharing every little setback and success of your family history research as it happens! Think of a blog as your family history research log. If this sounds appealing to you, you can learn the basics of starting your own family history blog in "*Blogging Your Family History Search*" (*http://genealogy.about.com/od/publishing/a/blogging.htm*) and learn even more from Thomas MacEntee's "*Genealogy Blog Primer*" (*www.geneabloggers.com/genealogy-blog-primer*).

Afterword

The Internet has definitely revolutionized genealogy. Computerized indexes make it possible to find individuals with very little information, on occasion without even a name. Digitized records make it possible to view page after page of records well into the wee hours, long after the library is locked up for the night. The availability of so many records in one place eliminates hours spent traveling to numerous repositories.

All of those benefits come with a price, however. Ease of publishing often results in half-done or shoddy research. The rush to put genealogical records online sometimes results in inaccurate indexes. The sheer wealth of available information makes finding the little bitty fact that you seek a very daunting task, but that information is out there, and you can find it! As you begin searching through the past, remember these basic dos and don'ts along the way. If you do, you're sure fill out your family tree in no time.

Do Look for Source Documentation

Just because you find information online doesn't mean that it's true. Before you accept any statement of fact, look for information on the original source of the information. Many online databases will include a source or "more about" link. Family trees will, hopefully, include contact information for the submitter. Be sure to document both this original source and the online source where you found the information, so you can accurately assess the quality of the information and so others can follow your research trail.

Don't Expect to Find Everything Online

Many people begin their genealogy search on the Internet expecting to find their entire family tree online, already completed back several centuries. The trouble is, it usually doesn't work that way. You can absolutely do a lot (or even a majority) of research online, but don't miss out on the fun and adventure of a visit to the local courthouse or family cemetery.

Do Your Homework Before Forking Over Your Money

Most of the commercial genealogy enterprises online are absolutely legitimate, but every now and then a website pops up with questionable business practices. Search the Internet for user comments and reviews of any website, software, or other commercial purchase before pulling out the credit card.

Don't Expect to Do It All for Free

You have probably noticed that certain subscription-based genealogy sites such as Ancestry.com keep coming up throughout this book. That's because even with the hefty price tag, these commercial subscription sites offer much more genealogical information online in one place than you'll find anywhere else. If you have a large family tree or plan to do a lot of research, a subscription will eventually pay for itself in time saved. If money is an issue, however, don't forget that many libraries offer free access to Ancestry Plus and/or HeritageQuest Online. You can also search out the many free databases and resources highlighted throughout this book.

Don't Publish Information on Living People Online

Your relatives probably won't be thrilled to find their birth dates and other private information online. Even just publishing their names along with the information on their parents can be too much, since many security systems use the mother's maiden name as identification. Use your genealogy software or a utility program to privatize this information before uploading your data online.

Don't Merge Family Trees

It's best to never import someone else's GEDCOM file directly into your own family tree. By taking time to enter the data into your genealogy software by hand, you get to learn about the new family connections. Otherwise you're letting software make all the decisions about who your ancestors are! If you do choose to import a GEDCOM file, however, make a backup of your main file first and import into the backup. This way you can revert back to your original file if the import has unanticipated results.

Do Give Back to the Genealogy Community

When you're first starting out, people will likely help you. After you've gained some experience, say thank you by helping someone else. Answer questions on a mailing list or forum. Do a few record lookups. Take time out to transcribe or index some records.

Don't Assume That Information on the Internet Is Public Domain

The majority of the articles, databases, transcriptions, and other genealogy information that you find online are protected by the copyright of the author. If you wish to repost such information in a blog, or on a mailing list or website, you need to get the author's permission. Acknowledging the source of the copyrighted material does not substitute for obtaining permission. For mailing lists and blogs, the best course of action is to use a small excerpt (considered "fair use") along with attribution to the author and a link to the original content.

Do Back Up Your Data on a Regular Basis

Since this was just discussed earlier in Chapter 12, hopefully it's still fresh in your mind. You do not want to lose hundreds of hours of genealogy research or irreplaceable family photos because you haven't backed up your digital files. Find a backup plan that works for you and stick to it.

And Finally . . . Don't Give Up

While the Internet exponentially increases your opportunities for locating your ancestors, it can also be an extremely frustrating experience to find just the right search combination. Use the search techniques introduced throughout this book and practice, practice, practice. It won't be long before you'll feel like a pro!

Appendix:
Further Readings

In addition to the books referenced throughout this work you may also find the following books helpful:

Ancestral Trails: The Complete Guide to British Genealogy and Family History, 2nd rev. ed., by Mark D. Herber (Baltimore, MD: Genealogical Publishing Co., 2006).

A comprehensive book on British genealogy and family history with information for the beginner and advanced researcher alike. This excellent book begins with the basics of starting your family tree, and then walks you through the maze of British records and repositories. There is some Internet coverage, but this is still primarily a guide to offline, published sources.

Ancestry's Red Book: American State, County and Town Sources, 3rd rev. ed., edited by Alice Eichholz, PhD (Provo, UT: Ancestry Publishing, 2004).

If you need to know when a particular county was formed, what records are available, or where records are kept, this reference book will generally have the answers, with resources and historical information organized by state and county. The previous edition is searchable online for anyone with a subscription to Ancestry.com.

Digitizing Your Family History: Easy Methods for Preserving Your Heirloom Documents, Photos, Home Movies, and More in Digital Format by Rhonda R. McClure (Cincinnati, OH: Family Tree Books, 2004).

If technology intimidates you a bit, this book will help you tackle the project of digitizing your family history, from choosing a scanner or digital camera to using software to fix up your old family photos or preserve your old family movies.

Evidence Explained: Citing History Sources from Artifacts to Cyberspace by Elizabeth Shown Mills (Baltimore, MD: Genealogical Publishing Co., 2007).

While there is no one proper method for citing your genealogy sources, many of us like to have a reference guide to offer examples and help point us in the right direction. Evidence Explained offers just that, with citation examples and models for thousands of different reference materials, from Internet databases and images to census records and court records. Elizabeth Mills also shares her expert guidance in how to analyze for yourself what the essential citation elements are for different types of records that you may encounter.

Hidden Sources: Family History in Unlikely Places by Laura Szucs Pfeiffer (Orem, UT: Ancestry Publishing, 2001).

Another excellent book geared toward getting you past your brick walls by introducing you to the vast variety of records in which you might discover your ancestors.

Land and Property Research in the United States by E. Wade Hone (Salt Lake City, UT: Ancestry Publishing, 1997).

Land records are among the oldest and best-preserved records available to American genealogists, but the variety of available land records and property laws can make them confusing to beginning researchers. This book is one to turn to again and again for land and property research.

Producing a Quality Family History by Patricia Law Hatcher (Salt Lake City, UT: Ancestry Publishing, 1996).

This excellent guide walks you through every step of producing a published family history of your family, including organizing your information; writing the narrative; and finalizing all of the little details, from choosing a typeface to creating a bibliography.

Professional Genealogy: A Manual for Researchers, Writers, Editors, Lecturers, and Librarians edited by Elizabeth Shown Mills (Baltimore, MD: Genealogical Publishing Co., 2001).

This comprehensive manual for professional genealogists is also a must-have for the serious hobbyist. Twenty-three chapters cover a variety of genealogical skills and standards, each presented by a professional genealogist with expertise in the subject. Topics include every aspect of professional genealogy, including proof standards and ethics and operating a genealogy business, plus family history research and publication.

Reading Early American Handwriting by Kip Sperry (Baltimore, MD: Genealogical Publishing Co., reprinted 2008).

Kip Sperry explains techniques for reading early American documents, provides samples of common alphabets and letter forms, and defines many of the unusual terms and abbreviations that you'll encounter. Numerous examples make it easy to practice what you've learned.

The BCG Genealogical Standards Manual by the Board for Certification of Genealogists (Orem, UT: Ancestry Publishing, 2000).

If you're interested in becoming a professional genealogist, or just want to produce a quality, well-researched family history, this official manual from the Board for Certification of Genealogists brings together a wide array of research standards, along with examples of how to put them into practice.

The Family Tree Problem Solver: Proven Methods for Scaling the Inevitable Brick Wall by Marsha Hoffman Rising (Cincinnati, OH: Family Tree Books, 2005).

When you hit a brick wall in your genealogy research, this book often comes to the rescue. The well-respected author offers a number of "brick wall" research techniques, along with case studies to demonstrate the techniques in action. She then delves into the most common types of genealogical research dead ends—missing records, ancestors who lived prior to 1850, and men with the same name—and the best ways to deal with them.

The Researcher's Guide to American Genealogy, 3rd ed., by Val D. Greenwood (Baltimore, MD: Genealogical Publishing Co., 2000).

Another essential reference for researchers in American genealogy, The Researcher's Guide identifies various classes of records used in genealogical research and tells where they are located and how to use them in research. This is both a reference book on available American records and a guide to the genealogical research process.

The Source: A Guidebook of American Genealogy, 3rd ed., edited by Loretto Dennis Szucs and Sandra Hargreaves Luebking (Provo, UT: Ancestry Publishing, 2006).

The Source is one of those books that exist on just about every professional genealogist's bookshelf. Each chapter, written by an expert, covers a different body of genealogy research, showing what sources are available, how to find them, and how to use them. This is the definitive book for anyone researching American genealogy. The previous edition is searchable online for anyone with a subscription to Ancestry.com.

Trace Your Roots with DNA: Using Genetic Tests to Explore Your Family Tree by Megan Smolenyak and Ann Turner (Emmaus, PA: Rodale Books, 2004).

Genetics and DNA are science, so you can expect to have to stretch your brain a little to really grasp how the tests work and how they can be used in conjunction with traditional genealogy research to learn more about your ancestors. While this book isn't exactly light reading given the subject matter, it is a very user-friendly introduction written by two experts in the field.

Uncovering Your Ancestry Through Family Photographs by Maureen A. Taylor (Cincinnati, OH: Family Tree Books, 2005).

It takes practice and experience to learn how to find the little clues hidden in your family photos that can help you identify the people, place, or time period. Author Maureen Taylor specializes in this area, and shares that expertise in this book, along with beautiful photographs to illustrate her points.

Unlocking Your Genetic History: A Step-by-Step Guide to Discovering Your Family's Medical and Genetic Heritage by Thomas H. Shawker (Nashville, TN: Rutledge Hill Press, 2004).

If you want to dig even further into the science behind the application of DNA testing for genealogy, Thomas Shawker also does an outstanding job of explaining this difficult subject in layman's terms. Especially important are the chapters on why it is important for you to know about your family's health history and how to compile and interpret your own medical pedigree.

You Can Write Your Family History by Sharon DeBartolo Carmack (Cincinnati, OH: Betterway Books, 2003).

This book is guaranteed to inspire almost anyone, even those of you who may not like to write, to successfully chronicle the fascinating tales of your ancestors. Her advice is practical and down-to-earth, taking you step by step through the process from researching to writing.

Index